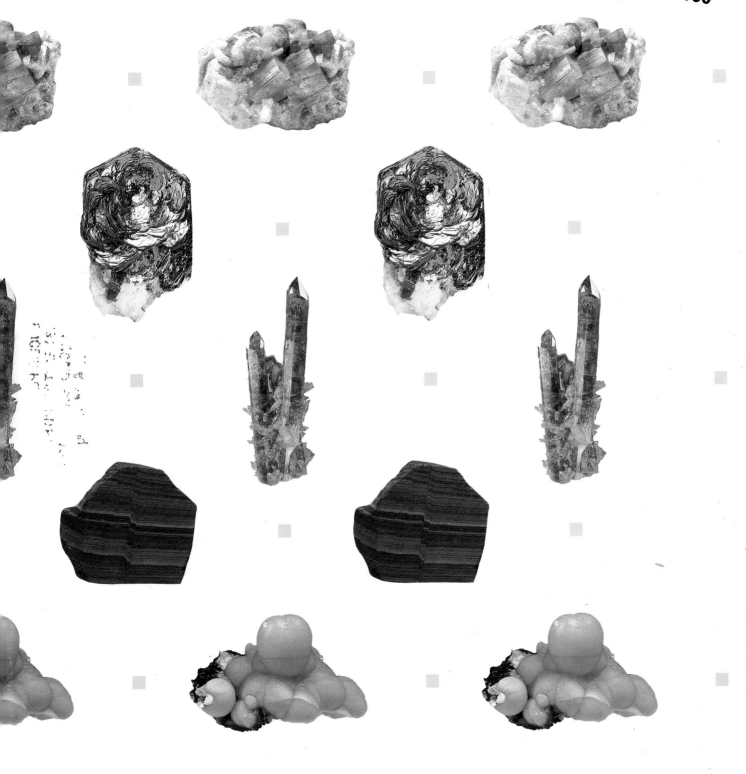

Hardness Bar Scale

There is one of these bar scales beside each of the minerals shown on pages 46 to 75. The harder the mineral, the higher the color rises. In this example the mineral has a hardness factor of 5 (see page 44 for an explanation of the Mohs Hardness Scale).

SCIENCE NATURE GUIDES

ROCKS & MINERALS
OF THE WORLD

Michael O'Donoghue

EDITED BY
Theodore Rowland-Entwistle

Silver Dolphin

Conservation

Rocks and minerals are not as easily damaged as a wild flower or a butterfly or a gopher, but they can still be destroyed. Every time we cut a path through a hillside for a new road or open a mine or build a dam, we are changing a landscape which has taken hundreds of thousand of years to make. We also change the way that trees, plants, insects, and animals live in that landscape. Some can adapt to the new conditions, but many cannot. Then another colony of butterflies, or a clump of orchids, or a beaver lodge will disappear for ever.

Of course, new roads and dams and mines sometimes have to be built, but it is important that the builders preserve as much as possible of what was there before. On page 76, you will find the names of some organizations who campaign against unnecessary destruction of the landscape. By joining them and supporting their efforts, you can help to preserve our world and all its creatures.

Rock Collectors' Code

1 **Always go collecting with a friend**, and always tell an adult where you have gone.
2 **Don't damage the site** and don't take more than one specimen of each rock—leave something for other collectors.
3 **Wear a hard hat** if you are exploring near a cliff. Check the cliff face carefully before you go near it, because loose rocks sometimes fall on people.
5 **Ask permission before exploring** quarries, sites on private land, or anywhere that you think belongs to somebody else.
5 **Leave fence gates as you find them**.
6 **Take your litter home**. Don't leave it to pollute the countryside.

Silver Dolphin Books
5880 Oberlin Drive
Suite 400
San Diego, CA 92121 - 9653

First published in the United States by Thunder Bay Press, 1994
Reprinted 1994
© Dragon's World, 1994
© Text Dragon's World, 1994
All rights reserved

Complete Cataloging in Publication (CIP) is available through the Library of Congress.
LC Card Number: 93–46148

The author and publishers would like to thank Dr Joel Arem and Dr Wendell E. Wilson for loaning the majority of the photographs illustrating this book.
© 1993 Wendell W. Wilson: 37BR, BL, 48, 49TL, BL, 48TR, BR, 49 TR, BL, BR, 50TL, B, 51TR, BL, BR, 52TL, BL, BR, 53TL, TR, 54, 55TR, B, 56TR, BL, 57T, 60, 61T, 62B, 63B, 64TL, TR, 65T, 67TL, B, 68TL, B, 69TR, BL, 70TR, 71TR, B, 72TL, BL, 73TR, BR, 74TR, 75.
© 1993 Joel Arem: 13–19, 20, 24–5, 28–33, 36–7, 40–1, 47TR, BR, 48TL, BL, 49TL, 50TR, 51TL, 52TR, 53BL, BR, 55TL, 56TL, BR, 57B, 61B, 62T, 63T, 64BL, 65B, 66, 67TL, 68TR, 69TL, BR, 70TL,B, 71TL, 72TR, BR, 73TL, BL, 74TL, BL, BR.
By courtesy of Natural History Museum, London: pages 20/21, 26/27.
By courtesy of Dr John D. Murray: pages 10/11, 38/39.
Explanatory illustrations by Ed Stuart; activity illustrations by Richard Coombes; headbands by Antonia Phillips.

Simplified text and captions written by Theodore Rowland-Entwistle, based on *An Illustrated Guide to Rocks and Minerals* by Michael O'Donoghue.

Editor	Diana Briscoe
Designer	James Lawrence
Design Assistant	Victoria Furbisher
Editorial Director	Pippa Rubinstein

Printed in Italy

ISBN 1-57145-379-2

Contents

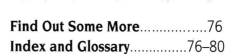

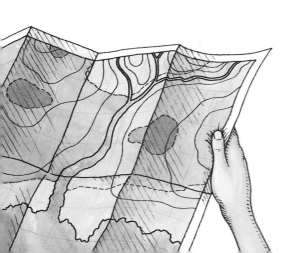

Introduction

Rocks are everywhere you go—houses and offices are built from them. You'll see them by the roadside, as pebbles on the beach, in cliffs and exposed on mountains. They are the raw materials of bricks and concrete. Tiny fragments of rock make up part of the soil in which plants grow.

More importantly, rocks shape the world we live in. If you understand rocks, you know why the landscape is the shape it is. You can understand why some soil is good for growing plants and some is not.

How this book works

This book is divided into two halves. **Rocks** (page 10) shows you the three main types of rocks and how they have made the many different landscapes of the world. You can also find out where to go and see the best examples of these landscapes.

Minerals (page 38) shows you the most common minerals and tells you where they can be found. They are grouped by the type of rock in which they are found. So, if you have igneous rocks in your neighborhood, you can see which minerals you are likely to find there.

You can go looking for mineral specimens but you may also get some of your mineral specimens from a rock store, or museum shop. If you want to check your specimens to see what they are, you can find out how to test them on pages 44–45.

You can see which rocks and minerals belong to which group by looking at the picture band at the top of each page. These bands are also shown under the picture on this page.

The first rocks

The earth is about 4,600 million years old. The oldest rocks that have been found were created by volcanic eruptions over hundreds of millions of years. These rocks are still being made every time a volcano erupts. They are called **igneous rocks**, from a Latin word meaning "like fire."

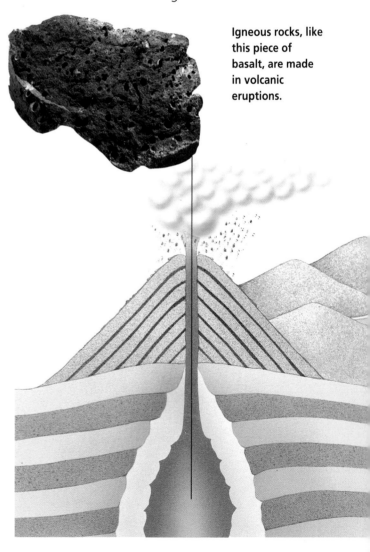

Igneous rocks, like this piece of basalt, are made in volcanic eruptions.

Igneous

Rocks from the sea

Over the years, water and wind gradually wear down these igneous rocks. The rocks break up into small pieces, called sediments, which are carried down rivers into the sea. The pieces come to rest deep under the sea and form sedimentary layers.

There is enormous pressure from the weight of the water on the sea bed. Under this pressure the sediments lower down in the sandwich layers are compressed into new rocks, called **sedimentary rocks**. Again, this takes many millions of years.

Sedimentary rocks, like this piece of sandstone, are made under the sea by pressure.

Altered rocks

Another group of rocks is created when existing igneous and sedimentary rocks are subjected to great heat and pressure. Such rocks are called **metamorphic rocks**, because their mineral ingredients have been changed.

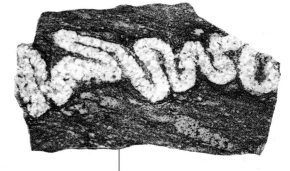

Metamorphic rocks, like this piece of migmatite, are made when igneous or sedimentary rocks are heated and/or squashed.

 **Sedimentary**

 **Metamorphic**

How Rocks Move About

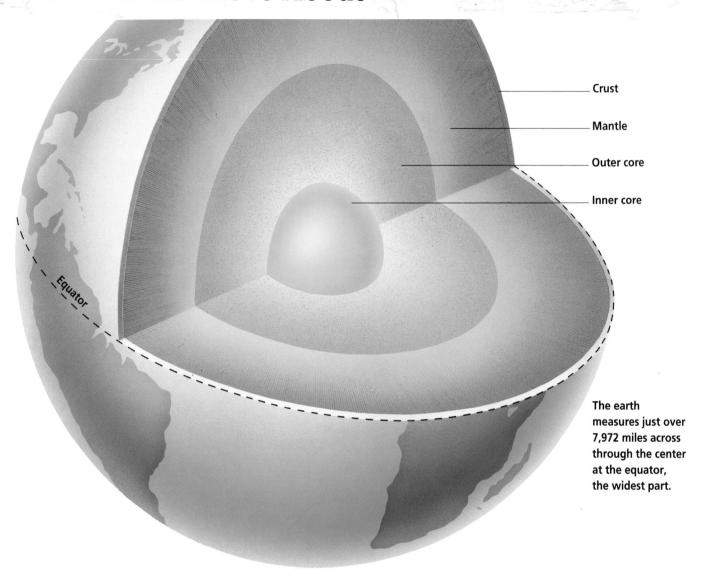

Crust

Mantle

Outer core

Inner core

Equator

The earth measures just over 7,972 miles across through the center at the equator, the widest part.

Did you know that fossilized fish have sometimes been found on top of mountains? To discover how this could happen, you have to look at what goes on under the earth's crust.

The **crust** (the outermost layer or skin) of the earth is very thin compared with the rest of it. On a school globe 1 foot across, the crust would be no thicker than a sheet of paper. In actual fact, the crust is about 25 miles thick under the continents, but only about 5 miles thick under the oceans.

Under the surface

Immediately below the crust is the **mantle**, which is a very thick layer of rock. It is about 1,810 miles thick. As you go in toward the center, the temperature gradually gets hotter. Inside the mantle is the **outer core**, probably made of molten iron and nickel. It is about 1,400 miles thick. The **inner core** is probably a solid ball of iron and nickel about 1,600 miles across. Its temperature is about 9,000° Fahrenheit (water's boiling point is 212° Fahrenheit).

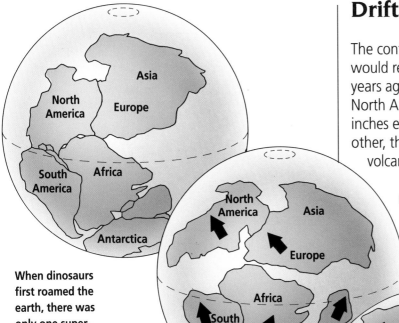

Drifting continents

The continents only moved into the pattern that we would recognize as today's world about 65 million years ago, and they are still moving. For example, North America and Europe move apart about 2 inches every year. When the plates collide with each other, there are earthquakes and volcanic eruptions.

Over many hundreds of millions of years mountains have been pushed up and worn away as the plates move backwards and forwards. Bits of the land have been pushed under the sea and later returned to the surface. New rocks have been formed and old ones have been metamorphosed (changed). How this happens is explained on the following pages.

When dinosaurs first roamed the earth, there was only one super-continent called Pangaea.

About 150 million years ago, the super-continent split into two smaller ones. They then split again into smaller sections.

About 100 million years ago, the continents were drifting toward the pattern we know today. Africa is about to collide with Europe.

The continents of North and South America joined up about 65 million years ago. This was shortly after the dinosaurs became extinct.

The changing earth

The crust of the earth is cold and hard but not fixed. The crust and the upper part of the mantle are divided into sections called plates and they move about very slowly, carrying the continents on which we live with them. They float on the hotter and more liquid rocks of the mantle below them.

About 200 million years ago, all the continents were joined together in a super-continent we call Pangaea. This broke up, first into two smaller super-continents, Laurasia and Gondwanaland, and then into the continents we know today.

Weather at work

Rock formations and mountains appear on the earth's surface as a result of things happening inside the earth. But they are sculpted into the shapes we see by the action of wind, water, and ice. This process is called erosion.

Water

Water is the most important means of erosion. It is drawn up from the sea by the heat of the sun, and then falls on the land as rain or snow. Then it flows back to the sea through rivers. As it passes over rocks, the water gradually wears them away.

Rocks wear away at different rates, but even the hardest rock can be eroded by water over a long time. In a river bed, lumps of rock tumble against one another as the water carries them along. They wear into smooth pebbles, and eventually into fine gravel, and then into sand or mud.

The sea also plays a large part in shaping the land. It crashes onto the shore, often driven by storm-force winds. It cuts away the bottom of cliffs, so the upper part falls onto the beach. There the waves slowly smash the rocks to pieces.

Wind power

When sand and fine soil are exposed to the wind, they may be blown about. Sand dunes are formed in this way. They are always changing in shape and can move great distances. Wind also drives the rain harder onto exposed rock and so helps the water to erode it faster. This spectacular example of wind erosion is in Utah.

How is soil made?

Soil is made from the very finest rock fragments (mud or sand) which are then mixed with humus. Humus is the dark brown material formed when plants and the bodies of insects and small animals decay. The humus fills the spaces between the rock particles.

Soil varies according to the sort of rock it is made from. For example, sandy soils come from sandstone, and chalky soils from limestone. Black sand comes from eroded igneous rock.

Plants need humus to survive. It feeds them and supplies them with water. Sand beaches have very little humus and so few plants grow there.

Volcanoes

A volcano is an opening in the Earth's crust through which the magma (molten rock) escapes from the Earth's interior. A volcano which often erupts, like Mount St. Helens in Washington, is said to be active.

A volcano that has not erupted for a long time is said to be dormant or inactive. Some volcanoes have not erupted for thousands of years, like Aconcagua in Argentina; they are said to be extinct. The vent of an extinct volcano is filled with cooled lava, which becomes solid rock and is called a plug.

How do volcanoes erupt?

Magma is pushed up from below the Earth's crust. When it finds a weak spot in the crust, it bursts through to form a volcano. Volcanoes produce several kinds of material: lava, rock fragments, ash, dust and gas. Lava is the molten magma—it flows out in a glowing, sticky mass, cooling as it comes into contact with the air.

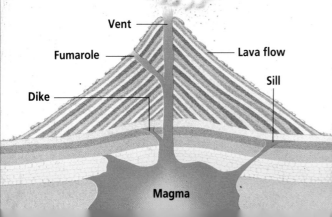

Vent

Fumarole

Lava flow

Sill

Dike

Magma

Where are the volcanoes?

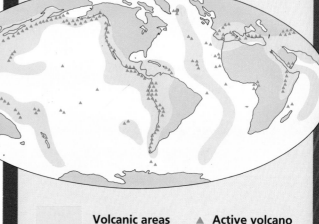

Volcanic areas ▲ Active volcano

Most volcanoes are found near the edges of the continental plates that cover the Earth (see page 7). Mount St. Helens, Washington, which erupted in 1980 and again since then, is close to the junction between the Pacific and the North American plates.

The ring of volcanoes all round the Pacific Ocean is sometimes called the Ring of Fire. There are also many volcanoes under the sea, particularly along the mid-ocean ridges.

Rocks from Volcanoes

These are called igneous rocks and they start as lava (igneous means fiery.) They are formed when molten magma from deep in the Earth cools in the open air. They are called extrusive rocks when they pour out of a volcano over the top of existing rocks.

Igneous rocks are the main rocks under the deep ocean beds. They are added to the Earth's crust at the underwater ocean ridges, like the mid-Atlantic Ridge. If the lava cools slowly, the texture of the final, solidified rock will be coarse and may include large crystals. If the lava cools quickly, it forms much finer-grained rocks.

Dikes and Sills

Not all magma comes to the surface. Sometimes it solidifies into a mass of granite deep underground —this is called a batholith. There is a huge batholith under the Sierra Nevada, California, and an even bigger one under the Coast Range in British Columbia, Canada. If the magma finds a horizontal crack in the crust, it may form a flat sheet of volcanic rock—this is called a sill. If the magma flows into a vertical crack, the result is called a dike.

A volcanic plug— the softer rocks around it have been eroded away by wind and rain, leaving the plug to stand alone.

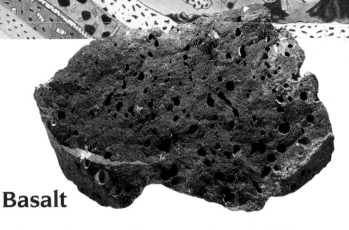

Andesite

Andesite is a typical rock of lava flows and volcanic environments. It is named for the Andes Mountains of South America, where there are major deposits of it. It is found all around the Pacific Ring of Fire, in the Sierra Nevada and Rocky Mountains, and in Japan. It is blackish-brown or green, with crystals of **biotite** and plagioclase **feldspar**. It is used as a building material. The mineral **copper** is sometimes found with andesite.

Obsidian

Obsidian is a rock made of natural glass. The glass forms because the magma has cooled very quickly, probably under the sea. It is usually gray to black, though it may have reddish streaks. Obsidian is found in lava flows dating from about 60 million years ago to today. In time it deteriorates into an ordinary looking, fine-grained rock. It is found in Italy, Hungary, and Japan. A spectacular outcrop is at Obsidian Cliff, in Yellowstone National Park. Obsidian is named after Obsius, a Roman who is said to have discovered the stone in Ethiopia.

Basalt

Basalt is a fine-grained igneous rock, mostly black, or very dark gray, or brown. It is found all around the world. It flows out from volcanoes to form large sheets, called traps. Large beds of it are found in North America around the Columbia and Snake Rivers and Lake Superior. It also is found under the sea, covered by mud and other sediments.

An unusual basalt formation is the Giant's Causeway in Northern Ireland. There the basalt has formed thousands of six-sided columns. Basalts are used for railroad and road ballast, and for making rock wool and fiberglass. The name comes through Latin from an African word for the rock.

Rhyolite

Rhyolite is formed when a very sticky magma cools rapidly. It is found in volcanic domes and chimneys. If it cools in contact with water, it forms small, pearly lumps known as Perlite, or Apache Tears. These are used ornamentally. Rhyolite is light in color; the black glassy variety is **obsidian**. There are major deposits of rhyolite in California and Oregon, Italy, eastern Europe, and Ethiopia. Its name comes from two Greek words meaning stream and stone.

Igneous Intrusions

Intrusive igneous rocks are ones that have been injected into existing country (original) rocks. They form batholiths, dikes, or sills (see page 10).

Anorthosite

Anorthosite is white or light gray, and has a granular texture. It is found in Norway, and is common over large areas of the Canadian Shield, in Newfoundland, Labrador, and the Adirondacks. It is named after **anorthite**—one of the plagioclase **feldspars** which form its main component. Some anorthosite is used for ornamental building stone.

Diorite

Diorite is the name given to several similar rocks which have as their main components **anorthite** and hornblende. Found in Minnesota, it is common in Scandinavia, France, Germany, and Romania. The rock has an overall grayish color. Polished slabs are used as building stone. The name comes from two Greek words meaning through a boundary.

Gabbro

Several igneous rocks are called gabbro. Most of them are coarse-grained and granular in texture. Their main component is plagioclase feldspar. Gabbros tend to be darker than diorite. Olivine gabbro is a variety in which **olivine** is a large component. Its color is gray with tinges of green, brown, or violet, and the grain size is medium. Few gabbros are usable as building stone, but olivine gabbro is an important source of olivine, and is the parent rock for some deposits of chromium, cobalt, iron, nickel, and **platinum** ores. The name comes from an Italian word meaning smooth or bald, used by marble workers near Florence, Italy.

Dunite

Dunite is composed mainly of the mineral **olivine**. From this comes its other name, olivine rock. It is a granular rock, light green in color. It is named for Mount Dun in New Zealand, where there are large deposits. It is also found in North Carolina, Turkey, where it contains chromium ore, and the Ural mountains, Russia, where it contains **platinum**.

Peridotite

Peridotite is a granular rock, and its grain size varies from fine to coarse.
Its color ranges from light to dark green, due to one of its main components, **olivine**. It is found world-wide, with large deposits in the United States, Canada, and South Africa. It is also found in the far south-west of England, and the Ural Mountains of Russia. It often occurs with deposits of metals such as nickel, chromium, and **platinum**.

Granite

Granite and similar rocks are the most common rocks on the Earth's continents. They form huge batholiths (see page 10). These masses of rock were originally below the earth's surface as in the Canadian Shield, and under Dartmoor, England. They also appear as sills and veins in other rocks. Their color ranges from white through light gray, pink, and pale yellow. The main components are **microcline**, **orthoclase**, plagioclase feldspars, and mica. The grain size is medium or fine. Granite is often used as a building stone. The name comes from the Latin word for a (wood) grained surface.

Syenite

Syenite is a medium-grained rock, ranging in color from gray through pink to violet. It is often found in association with granite. The main components include feldspars, **biotite**, and **diopside**, plus a small amount of **quartz**. It occurs in masses in New York, and in Norway, Germany, and Italy. It is often used as polished slabs in building. The name comes from Syrene in Egypt, where a similar rock containing much more quartz was first identified.

Kimberlite

Kimberlite is a form of **peridotite** (see above) which contains angular fragments. The grain size varies, but it is one of the main types of rock in which **diamonds** are found. It generally occurs as pipes—cylinder-shaped holes in the earth's crust. It is named after Kimberley, South Africa, one of the world's richest diamond areas. It is also found in the Rocky Mountains, the Canadian Shield, and Yakutskaya in Siberia. Its many component minerals include **olivine**, **garnet**, pyroxene, **diopside**, and **calcite**. Its color can be black, blue, greenish, or yellow.

Sedimentary Beds

The Earth is continually recycling its crust. As mountains are formed they are steadily worn away, and the fragments are washed down into lakes, rivers, and the sea. They are called sediments. There they settle to the bottom and build up layer upon layer of mud and sand. Over thousands of years these accumulated layers form new rocks, called sedimentary rocks.

The raw materials

The type of sediments from which these new rocks are formed, depends on the minerals that were in the original fragments. Some sediments are pieces of older rocks that have been worn away the weather. They include sand, which are mainly silica, and **clay**, which is aluminum silicate.

Rocks made entirely of sand are called **sandstones**. They were built up in lakes and estuaries, but some were originally loose sand blown into dunes by the wind. Other rocks are formed as the result of chemical action. Calcium and magnesium carbonates form limestones. Chalk beds, like those in Kansas, also contain the chalky skeletons of millions of tiny sea animals.

Sediments form successive layers called beds. When these layers become rock, geologists call them strata, which means layers. The loose material of the sediments are cemented together by minerals, and by pressure. The weight of the sea water may be enough to consolidate the material, but upheavals in the crust apply far more pressure.

The finest example of sedimentary beds can be seen in the Grand Canyon in Arizona. There, layers of different rocks more than one mile deep are exposed. The canyon has been cut by the waters of the Colorado River, but the land has also risen while the river has been flowing.

Sedimentary Rocks

Breccia

This is a mixture of angular rock fragments held together in a fine-grained natural cement. The fragments may be all of the same rock, or from many different rocks. It is often found in old landslides or as a result of the folding and fracturing of rocks. It is used as an ornamental building stone.

Conglomerate

This is made of lumps and pebbles of rock, sometimes of several kinds, in a fine-grained natural cement. When a gravel bed turns into rock, the result is conglomerate. It can be used for building. It is found in the eastern United States and South Africa. A variety with a muddy-looking cement binding the gravel together is called Pudding Stone.

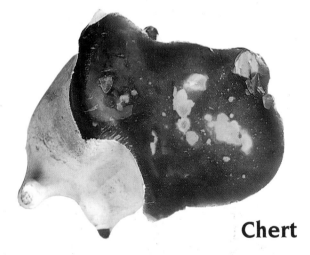

Chert

This occurs as nodules, when it is called flint (see picture), or as veins in other rocks. It is a mixture of silica with traces of **calcite** and other minerals. It often contains fossils of tiny marine animals, when it is called Radiolarite. Varieties include agate, chrysoprase, and onyx.

Dolomite

A soft, ultra-basic rock found in many places in the world but particularly in the Dolomite Mountains of Italy, Iowa, Michigan, Missouri, and Vermont. It is formed from **limestone**, coral, or **marble** by chemical changes caused by dissolved magnesium. Light gray or yellow in color, it is used for building.

Graywacke

This rock, a hard, grayish **sandstone**, is made from silt sediments that are deposited in deep water. It is dark gray or brown in color. It contains **quartz,** feldspar, and fragments of other rocks in a clayey matrix. It is found worldwide in thick bands.

Sandstone

This is the name of a group of sedimentary rocks made up of sand-sized grains. Most of the grains are silica. The grain size varies from 2 mm to 0.063 mm. Its color varies from white through gray, yellow, green, red to brown. One of the commonest sedimentary rocks, sandstone is used as a building material; the brownstone buildings of New York are built of sandstone. The cement binding the grains is usually **quartz**..

Clay

This name describes a group of very fine-grained rocks. Clay is soft and pliable when wet. When baked, it becomes hard and is used to make roof tiles, dishes, flower pots, and many other things that you will find in your home.

Shale forms in definite layers, and may fall to pieces when wet. Mudstones are similar to shales but without definite layers. Siltstones and Marl are varieties of mudstone.

Limestone Caves

All rain is slightly acid, even without human pollution. This acid in rainwater comes from carbon dioxide in the air, and will dissolve some types of rocks, particularly limestone or dolomite. However, most acid rain is caused by sulfur and nitrogen oxides. These are released into the air by industrial complexes, cars, and volcanic eruptions.

Limestone has vertical and horizontal faults in it. The water seeps along these cracks, gradually making them bigger. Water flowing through limestone may eventually form underground rivers. These rivers carve out magnificent caves, such as the Mammoth-Flint Ridge cave system in Kentucky, with more than 190 miles of caverns, passages, lakes, and rivers.

If water containing dissolved limestone trickles down the walls of a cave it forms a translucent layer; formed at a known rate, the thickness of the layer may be used to date a cave painting underneath it. That is how we know many of the cave paintings made by Stone Age people in caves in France and Spain are 20,000 or more years old.

Stalactites and Stalagmites

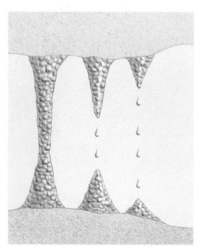

Water dissolves limestone as it seeps through it. As this water drips from the roof of a cave, it will (over hundreds of years) form a stalactite. Below the drip a stalagmite will rise from the floor. Sometimes they join up to make a pillar.

Limestone

This rock is made up mostly of calcium and carbon. It is formed under the sea, partly from the skeletons of tiny marine animals. The fossilized shells of other sea creatures and even large land animals also can be found in it. Limestone is used for building and for railroad ballast.

Limestone cave system

How caves grow

1 Limestone cliff with a network of cracks
2 Cave with a spring where stalactites and stalagmites are growing
3 Cave formed when the ceiling collapsed
4 Mound of rubble from the collapsed ceiling

5 Underground stream flowing from the spring
6 Cave with a lake. At one time the river would have flowed out of the
7 Cave entrance
8 Underground river flowing out of the lake and reaching the open air as a waterfall down the cliff

Find Out About Limestone

Stalactites can grow anywhere that the water is hard, even in your own home. The hardness or softness of your water depends on what kinds of rock and soil the water has flowed through after it fell as rain.

Testing for hard water

Hard water contains calcium bicarbonate, which has dissolved out of a limestone, like chalk. When ordinary water is boiled, the calcium bicarbonate is converted into calcium carbonate (**calcite**). This is what stalactites and stalagmites are made from (see page 20).

You can easily find out if your water is hard or soft, by seeing how well soap lathers in it. If it lathers well, then the water is soft. If it doesn't, the water is hard.

You can't try this with detergent, because it is chemically different from ordinary soap.

You can buy descalers for electric coffee-makers or shower heads which dissolve the "fur" away. Next time your mother descales something, ask if you can watch. You will see the limescale fizzing away from the sides. **Be careful not to breathe the fumes from the descaler—they will harm your lungs!**

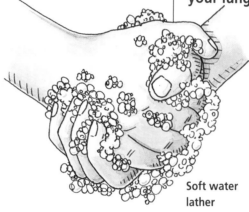

Soft water lather

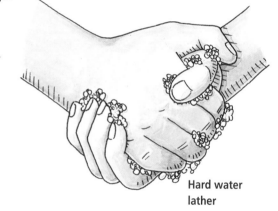

Hard water lather

Looking for stalactites

The best place to see stalactites is, of course, in a limestone cave. But even if you do not live close to a cave you can probably still find some stalactites near your home.

Look for an old bridge or short road tunnel where the ground above is very damp. The chances are that the water will drip through the bridge, especially if it is built of brick. If it does, tiny stalactites will grow on the underside of the bridge or tunnel, just as they would in a cave.

It's easy to remember the difference between the two! Stalac**tites** hold **tight** to the roof, while stalag**mites** **might** one day reach it.

Grow a stalactite

You can grow your own stalactites and stalagmites at home by following these instructions:

1 **Collect the following items:** a large mixing bowl, 2 large glass jelly jars, an old saucer, some wool, and a large packet of borax. (You can buy borax (washing soda) from a supermarket or grocery store.)
2 **Heat enough water** to fill the two jars and pour it into the mixing bowl—the hotter, the better. Add the borax slowly, stirring as you go, until it won't dissolve any more crystals.
3 **Pour the mixture into the jars** and stand them about 10 ins apart on a flat surface. Put the saucer between them.
4 **Make a rope** by twisting or braiding 10 or 12 pieces of wool together. It should be about 2 ft long. Sink one end into each jar, so that it forms a gentle curve between the jars with the lowest point over the saucer.
5 **Leave the jars and thread** set up for 4–5 days. The solution of water and borax is absorbed up the rope from each jar and then along the loop. You will find that little stalactites form in the center as the water dries from the rope. Some of the water will drip into the saucer and a tiny stalagmite will start to grow underneath.

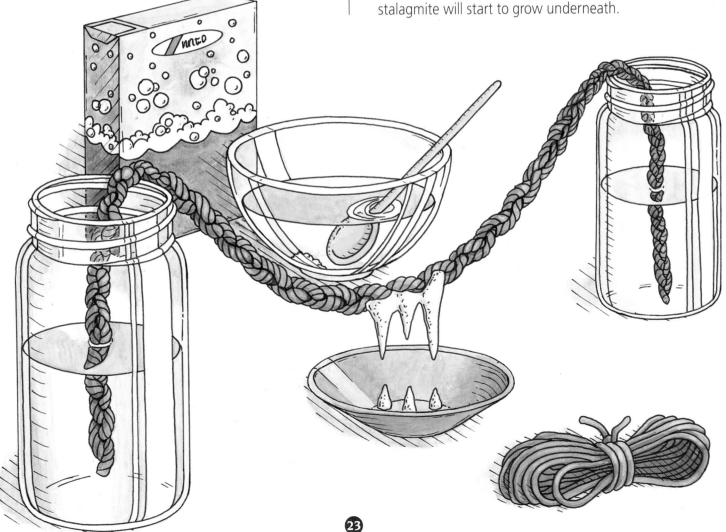

Rocks in Rivers

Many sandstones are the result of material deposited in rivers. Moving water carries tiny rock fragments suspended in it. As the river goes round a bend the fragments settle on the downhill side of the slope, where the water moves more slowly.

A river bed may contain many different kinds of rocks, particularly in a mountainous region. Most of the boulders will have been there before the river started flowing. They will look rounded because they have been eroded by the river. Other rocks will have been carried down from higher upstream.

Rivers wash material out of rocks and gravels and this has helped people to find **gold**. Fine grains of gold, and sometimes bigger lumps called nuggets, have been found in or near rivers in many parts of the world. Deposits that contain useful quantities of valuable minerals, such as **diamonds**, **gold**, **platinum**, and tin, are called placer deposits, from a Latin-American word meaning sandbank.

Because the minerals are heavier than the rest of the sand and gravel in the river bed, they can be separated by panning—washing them in a shallow pan. The lighter material rinses away, leaving the heavier minerals behind.

Placer formation

A river picks up sediments and rocks as it flows down toward the sea.

As the river goes round a curve, it drops sediments on its downhill side, forming a placer.

Next the water starts eroding the downhill bank at the end of one bend and the uphill bank at the start of the next.

As more sediments are dropped, the bends get bigger and bigger.

The bends get more and more curved, until eventually they join.

The river drops sediments in a different place. This cuts off a bit of its bed to make a little lake, while the river runs straight again.

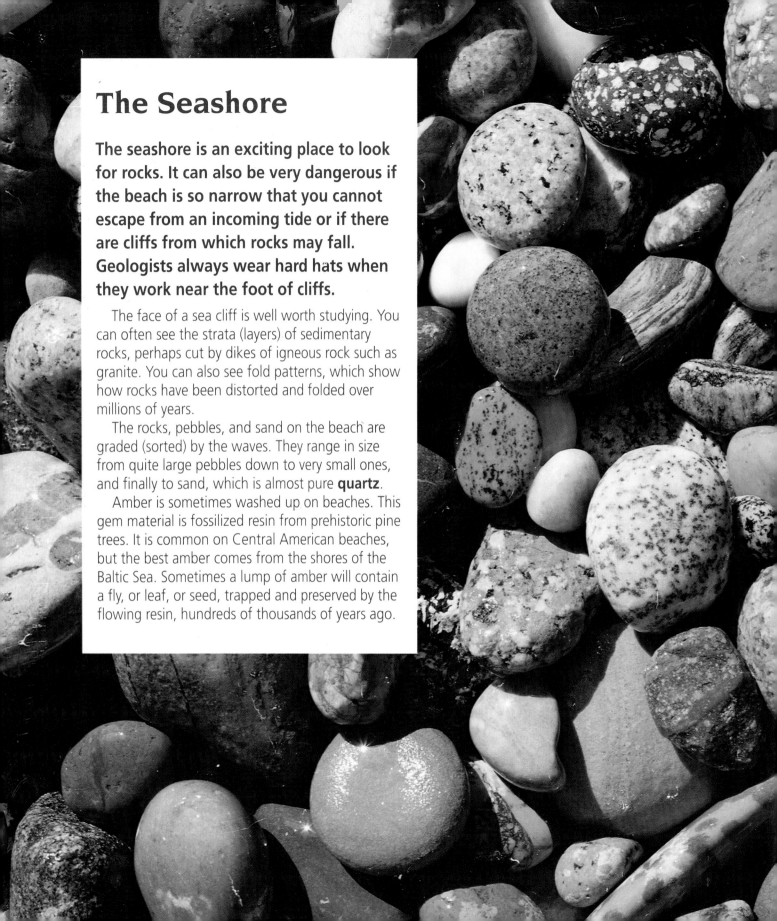

The Seashore

The seashore is an exciting place to look for rocks. It can also be very dangerous if the beach is so narrow that you cannot escape from an incoming tide or if there are cliffs from which rocks may fall. Geologists always wear hard hats when they work near the foot of cliffs.

The face of a sea cliff is well worth studying. You can often see the strata (layers) of sedimentary rocks, perhaps cut by dikes of igneous rock such as granite. You can also see fold patterns, which show how rocks have been distorted and folded over millions of years.

The rocks, pebbles, and sand on the beach are graded (sorted) by the waves. They range in size from quite large pebbles down to very small ones, and finally to sand, which is almost pure **quartz**.

Amber is sometimes washed up on beaches. This gem material is fossilized resin from prehistoric pine trees. It is common on Central American beaches, but the best amber comes from the shores of the Baltic Sea. Sometimes a lump of amber will contain a fly, or leaf, or seed, trapped and preserved by the flowing resin, hundreds of thousands of years ago.

Pebble beaches

The kinds of pebbles on a beach depend on the rocks nearby. In a high cliff there may be several kinds of rock. As lumps fall down and are worked on by the waves they turn into pebbles.

Igneous rocks are more likely to turn into pebbles than many sedimentary rocks, because they are much harder and do not wear away so readily. For example, in **granite** country you will find pink or gray mottled pebbles, while **basalt** country produces black pebbles.

In chalk regions many of the pebbles will be of **flint**. They may not be obvious, because they develop a softish brown coating, which hides the hard, dark gray rock inside. You can also sometimes find small stone balls, about the size of a ping-pong ball, which are much heavier than other pebbles. They are **pyrite** nodules.

A few pebbles appear to be valuable green or brown gemstones, but they are usually colored glass, probably from old bottles, that have been broken up and smoothed into pebbles. Bricks and lumps of concrete may also be worn into pebbles.

Metamorphic Rocks

Metamorphic rocks are those which have been changed inside the Earth's crust by heat, pressure, and chemical activity. Both igneous and sedimentary rocks can be metamorphosed, a word which means changed completely.

Some rocks are metamorphosed over thousands of square miles. This happens when rocks that have been buried deep in the Earth return to the surface through earthquakes or the erosion of the rocks above them. This process is known as regional metamorphism.

Contact metamorphism occurs in rocks that lie close to where new igneous rocks have been thrust up to the surface. This heats the existing rocks up and changes them. Contact metamorphism is often found in the rock surrounding a dike.

Many metamorphic rocks, like gneisses, can be easily identified by their striped or banded appearance. They are formed under considerable pressure.

Metamorphic Rocks

Hornfels

Hornfels is a contact metamorphic rock, derived from clays. The main minerals include **quartz**, **feldspars**, **andalusite**, and **biotite**. The color may be pink, brown, violet, or green. Hornfels contains crystals enclosing other crystals of different minerals. It occurs in the Sierra Nevada, California, Scotland, Norway, and France. It doesn't have a particular use. Its name comes from a German word meaning horn rock, referring to its luster.

Marble

Marble is formed by both regional and contact metamorphism. The parent rock is **limestone**, recrystallized, and the main mineral is **calcite**. The colors vary from pure white to a mosaic of red, green, or brown streaks, and patches. Marble is found all over the world, sometimes in huge quantities such as the 80-mile long bed in Vermont, which contains marbles of several different colors. The most famous marble comes from Carrara in Italy. It has been used by sculptors for hundreds of years. The name marble comes from a Greek word meaning to sparkle.

Skarn

Skarn is formed by the metamorphism of **limestones** in contact with **granites**. Volatile fluids containing boron, chlorine, and fluorine take iron, magnesium, manganese, and silicon from the granitic rock into the limestone to form new minerals. It is common in the United States, and also in Great Britain, Sweden, Japan, and parts of Central and South America. Skarn is often a source rock for **copper**, iron, manganese, and molybdenum. The origin of the name is uncertain.

Slate

Slate is a contact metamorphic rock, and the parent sedimentary rocks are mostly **clays** or shales. The main minerals include **andalusite**, **biotite**, and **muscovite**. It is found world-wide, especially in the Sierra Nevada, California, and in Great Britain, Norway, Finland, and France. Slate is usually gray or black. It splits easily into thin sheets which are used for roofing, and as flagstones. The name comes from an Old French word meaning to splinter.

Gneiss

Gneiss is a regional metamorphosed rock. The parent rocks are often sedimentary, but some gneisses have formed from granite-like igneous rocks. The main minerals include feldspars, **biotite**, and **muscovite**. Gneiss is coarse-grained, with irregular banding. The color varies from light, in gneisses derived from **granite**, to dark, in rocks derived from **sandstones**. Gneiss occurs world-wide. There are good deposits in New York, New England, Georgia, and the Rocky Mountains; in Europe it is common throughout the Alps. It is sometimes used as a building stone. The name comes from an old German word meaning to give off sparks.

Schist

Schist is the name given to a variety of regional metamorphic rocks, which vary according to the main minerals in them and the parent rocks. Schists can be identified by the parallel arrangement of most of their minerals. The name schist comes from a Greek word meaning to split.

Mica schists come from clay sedimentary rocks, and contain mica (**biotite** and **muscovite**) and **quartz**. Chlorite schists come from lava, and the main mineral is chlorite. Talc schist is greasy to the touch, like the mineral **talc** which is its main ingredient.

Quartzite

Quartzite is a regional metamorphic rock made up entirely or mostly of the mineral **quartz**, which is where it gets its name. The parent rocks are many kinds of quartz-rich sedimentary rocks, for example **graywacke** or **flint**. Pure quartzite is white, but if other minerals are present it may be gray—even black if dark minerals like **biotite** are included. It is found worldwide. There are large deposits in the Carolinas. It is found all over Scotland, India, and Brazil. Quartzite is used for floors and building facing stone, and also in glass and ceramics.

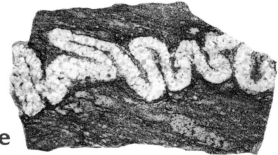

Migmatite

Migmatite is the name given to a type of composite rock which is a mixture of two pre-existing rocks. The country (original) rock is some kind of metamorphic rock which is remelted when it is invaded by either magma or a hydrothermal solution. The formation takes place far below the surface. Migmatites are found world-wide, in rocks more than 560 million years old. The origin of the name is uncertain. They are used as building stone.

Plants turn into Rocks

Coal is a soft rock, colored black or brown. Unlike ordinary rocks, it was formed from organic (living) material. It is the fossil remains of prehistoric plants, which is why coal is called a fossil fuel.

If coal deposits are close to the surface, strip mining is used. Powerful diggers strip away the soil and rock above the coal and heap it to one side. The coal is then dug away. Finally the land is restored as near as possible to its original condition.

Most coal seams lie deep underground. To reach them, miners must sink a shaft. Then tunnels are dug along the line of the seam. The miners are taken down to their work by elevator and the coal and spoil (waste rock) is brought up in it.

Coal is graded according to how old, and so how hard it is. Lignite, often called brown coal because of its color, is fairly young. There are large deposits of lignite in Pennsylvania and eastern Europe. Bituminous coal is the most common kind, and gives off most heat. It is the type mostly mined in the United States. The hardest coal is anthracite, which burns slowly with very little smoke.

This is anthracite coal, the blackest, hardest, and oldest of all.

Trees into coal

Lignite coal

Bituminous coal

Anthracite coal

Between 345 and 280 million years ago, in the Carboniferous Period, there were huge forests of giant ferns, growing in swampland.

When the tree ferns died they fell into the swampy ground, where they decayed to form a thick layer of partly rotted vegetation.

Over millions of years, as the continents moved and the climate altered, this rotting layer was covered with mud and sand.

This happened over and over again. The huge sandwich grew to be thousands of yards thick.

When the deeply buried layers of decayed vegetation were compressed and heated up, this changed them into seams of coal.

City Survey

You don't have to go on field trips to distant mountains to study rocks. There are lots of different rocks in your home town. Take a walk around the streets and you'll be amazed at how many there are.

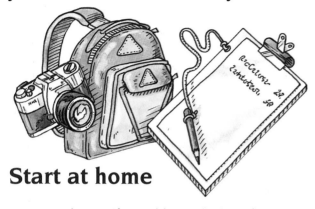

Start at home

Your own home, if it is old, may be built from stone, but it is more likely to be built of clay brick. If it is a wood-frame house it will have brick in the foundations. The roof may be clay tiles or **slates**.

When you look through a window, you are looking through rock. The glass in it is made from calcium, sodium, and silica.

Some older buildings are coated with stucco —this is a mixture of lime, sand, and water. If you find such a building, you can add the mineral **gypsum** (see page 53) to your list.

On Main Street

Now go out into your street. Have a look at the curbstones of the sidewalk. If they are not made of concrete, they are probably **granite** blocks.

You are likely to see many different rocks in the buildings in your main street. Many old buildings are made of **sandstone** or **limestone**, or if they were built in the last twenty years or so, they may be faced with slabs of those rocks.

If you go inside a bank or office, have a look at the floor. It may well be of **marble** or some other hard, decorative stone. Take a look at the steps of buildings you pass; they are often stone.

Hidden rocks

Don't forget the rocks that are hidden because they are made into other materials. There's the clay in bricks, for example. You probably can't identify the crushed granite or **basalt** in the road surface, but it's there all right.

Cement is a mixture of limestone, silica (from sand), and alumina (from clay). It is mixed with sand and lime to make mortar which holds the bricks together. It is also mixed with crushed rock or small pebbles (called aggregate) to form concretes. These are used to build skyscrapers.

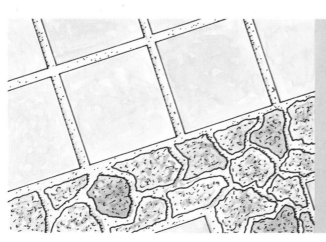

What about the garden?

Take a look in your yard or in the local park. If you have a patio, look to see what sort of slabs were used for the paving. They may be concrete, so you can put down cement and aggregate on your list. If they are stone, try to identify it. It will most likely be a sandstone. If there's a rock garden, have a close look at the rocks used to build it, and try to identify them.

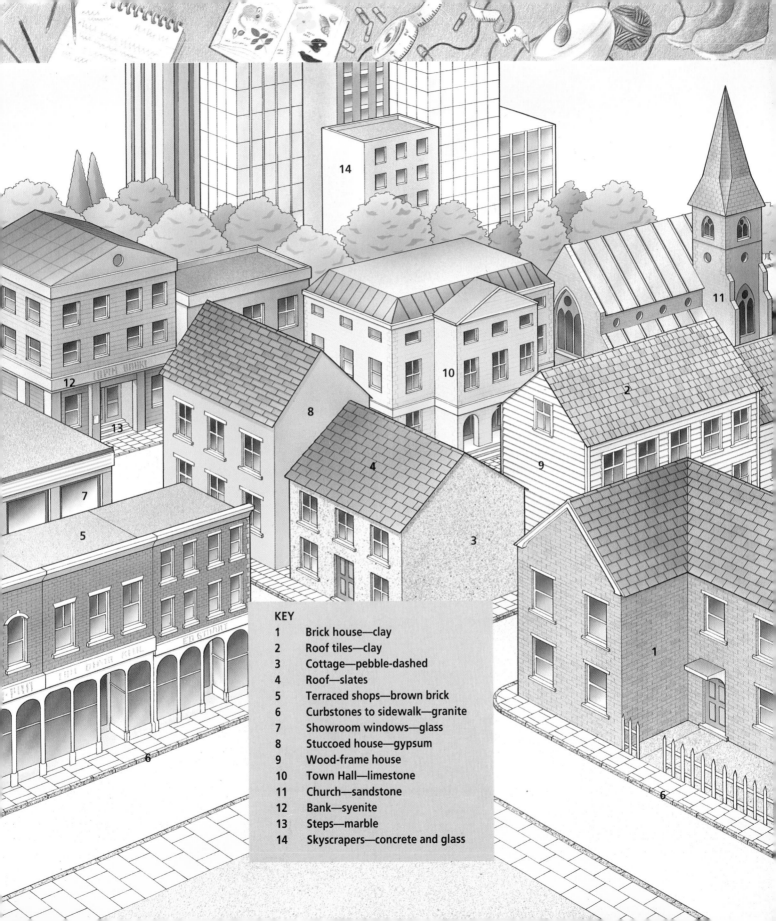

KEY

1 Brick house—clay
2 Roof tiles—clay
3 Cottage—pebble-dashed
4 Roof—slates
5 Terraced shops—brown brick
6 Curbstones to sidewalk—granite
7 Showroom windows—glass
8 Stuccoed house—gypsum
9 Wood-frame house
10 Town Hall—limestone
11 Church—sandstone
12 Bank—syenite
13 Steps—marble
14 Skyscrapers—concrete and glass

Rocks from the sky

Meteors are pieces of stone or metal from outer space which enter the Earth's atmosphere. Friction makes them grow hot and glow, causing the phenomenon called shooting stars.

Most meteors burn up, but about 10,000 tons of space rubble survives to reach the Earth's surface every year. Most of it is little more than dust, but about twenty lumps each year will weigh more than 2 lbs. These are called meteorites.

Giant meteors

A number of giant meteors have struck the Earth during its 4,600 million-year history. Most of the craters they caused have vanished because the Earth's surface has changed many times during that time. But you can see huge numbers of meteor craters on the Moon and some of the planets, because there has been no erosion to destroy the marks of the impact.

Some craters do survive on Earth, like Meteor Crater in Arizona (shown here) which is about 25,000 years old. It measures over 1,320 yds across and was made by a meteorite measuring about 100 yds wide. There is another huge crater in Siberia.

Larger objects from space have hit the Earth in the past. The element iridium is far more common in meteorites than in the Earth's own rocks, but a layer of iridium has been found under the sea. This is thought to have come from a small asteroid (minor planet) which hit the Earth about 65 million years ago. Its crater is believed to lie in the Gulf of Mexico, and its impact may have created a cloud of dust which led to the extinction of the dinosaurs.

Iron meteorite

Where do they come from?

All meteorites come from within the solar system—the planets, minor planets, and fragments that circle the Sun. There are two kinds. Stony meteorites are mostly non-metallic rock with particles of iron.

Iron meteorites are mostly iron and nickel, with small amounts of carbon, cobalt, **copper**, phosphorus, and **sulfur**. Meteoritic iron was the first kind that people used to work into tools and weapons. This started about 3,000 years ago, at the beginning of the Iron Age.

Stone meteorite

What are Minerals?

Just as rocks are the building blocks of the earth's crust, so minerals are the building blocks of rocks. Minerals are natural substances—they are inorganic (not originally part of a plant or animal).

Minerals are made from the chemical elements. There are ninety-two natural elements in the world (there are others that are man-made) and each contains atoms of just one unique type. Atoms are so small that over 20 billion of them would fit on the period at the end of this sentence.

Most minerals form in the magma (molten rock) far below the earth's surface. As the magma is pushed up toward the crust, it cools and then some of the elements begin to crystallize—they combine to form little solid blocks called crystals. Minerals crystallize at different temperatures and pressures within the magma. As a result, two or more minerals can contain bits of the same element, but put together in a different way.

Identifying minerals

There are several clues to identifying a mineral. They include its color, the shape of its crystals, its hardness, its specific gravity and streak. A chemist can also identify the chemical elements in each mineral. You can find out how to carry out these tests on pages 44–45. Each mineral shown in this book has a short data caption that tells you the identification details of that mineral. This will help you to check your specimens. A name in **bold** lettering shows that there is an entry for the rock or mineral in this book.

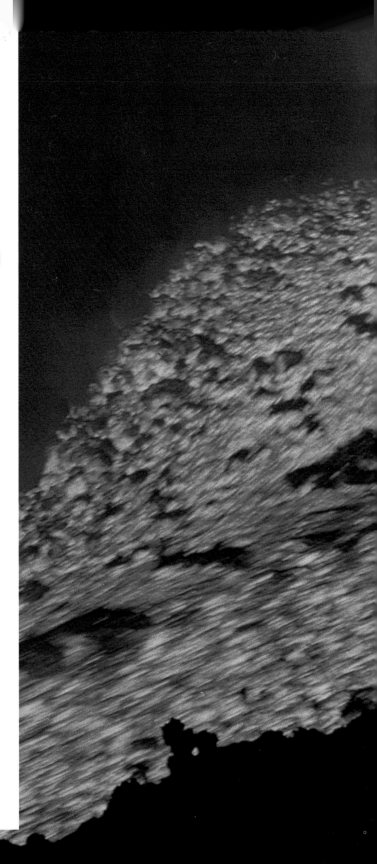

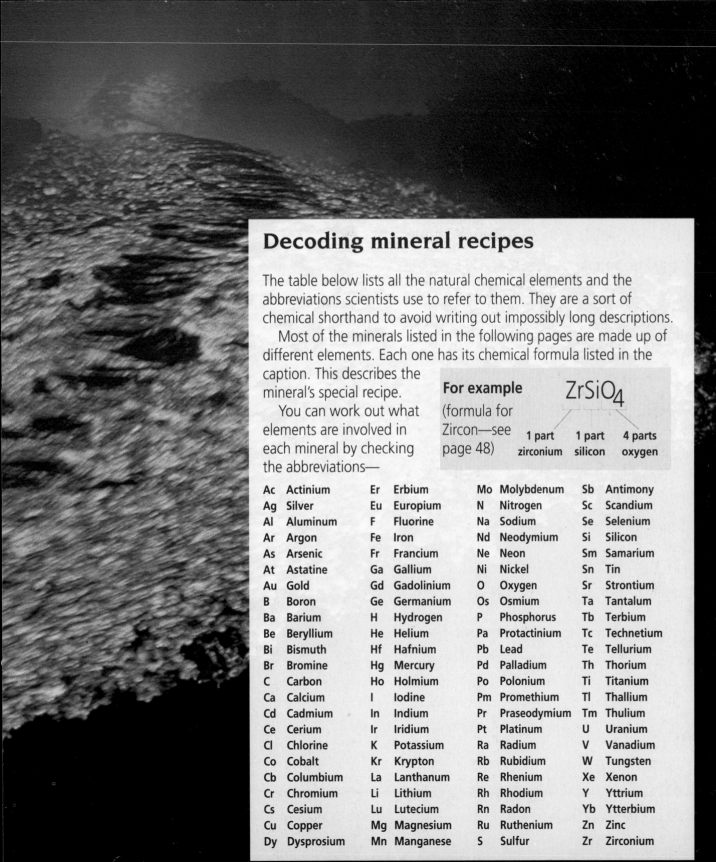

Decoding mineral recipes

The table below lists all the natural chemical elements and the abbreviations scientists use to refer to them. They are a sort of chemical shorthand to avoid writing out impossibly long descriptions.

Most of the minerals listed in the following pages are made up of different elements. Each one has its chemical formula listed in the caption. This describes the mineral's special recipe.

You can work out what elements are involved in each mineral by checking the abbreviations—

For example (formula for Zircon—see page 48)

$$ZrSiO_4$$

| 1 part zirconium | 1 part silicon | 4 parts oxygen |

Ac	Actinium	Er	Erbium	Mo	Molybdenum	Sb	Antimony
Ag	Silver	Eu	Europium	N	Nitrogen	Sc	Scandium
Al	Aluminum	F	Fluorine	Na	Sodium	Se	Selenium
Ar	Argon	Fe	Iron	Nd	Neodymium	Si	Silicon
As	Arsenic	Fr	Francium	Ne	Neon	Sm	Samarium
At	Astatine	Ga	Gallium	Ni	Nickel	Sn	Tin
Au	Gold	Gd	Gadolinium	O	Oxygen	Sr	Strontium
B	Boron	Ge	Germanium	Os	Osmium	Ta	Tantalum
Ba	Barium	H	Hydrogen	P	Phosphorus	Tb	Terbium
Be	Beryllium	He	Helium	Pa	Protactinium	Tc	Technetium
Bi	Bismuth	Hf	Hafnium	Pb	Lead	Te	Tellurium
Br	Bromine	Hg	Mercury	Pd	Palladium	Th	Thorium
C	Carbon	Ho	Holmium	Po	Polonium	Ti	Titanium
Ca	Calcium	I	Iodine	Pm	Promethium	Tl	Thallium
Cd	Cadmium	In	Indium	Pr	Praseodymium	Tm	Thulium
Ce	Cerium	Ir	Iridium	Pt	Platinum	U	Uranium
Cl	Chlorine	K	Potassium	Ra	Radium	V	Vanadium
Co	Cobalt	Kr	Krypton	Rb	Rubidium	W	Tungsten
Cb	Columbium	La	Lanthanum	Re	Rhenium	Xe	Xenon
Cr	Chromium	Li	Lithium	Rh	Rhodium	Y	Yttrium
Cs	Cesium	Lu	Lutecium	Rn	Radon	Yb	Ytterbium
Cu	Copper	Mg	Magnesium	Ru	Ruthenium	Zn	Zinc
Dy	Dysprosium	Mn	Manganese	S	Sulfur	Zr	Zirconium

Crystals

Crystals are minerals that have solidified into a shape with flat surfaces and a regular pattern of atoms (see page 38), as opposed to a bulgy mass. Almost all minerals form crystals in the right conditions: glass and opal are exceptions.

Many crystals grow from molten magma as it cools after it has been thrust up to the crust of the earth. Some crystals, such as salt, grow from solutions (substances dissolved in a liquid). Yet others form from the gases escaping from volcanoes—sulfur crystals are formed in this way.

Most gemstones used in jewelry have been cut from crystals. The complicated pattern of cuts, known as facets, are designed to show off the stone's color and sparkle to its best advantage.

Some crystals grow to enormous sizes. The huge gypsum crystals shown in the main picture are from the Cave of Swords at Naica in Mexico.

Crystal shapes

The best way to learn about crystal shapes is to look at as many examples as you can—for example in museums and rock stores. Their shapes are often simple, but very difficult to describe in words.

Crystals can be grouped into just seven basic types or systems, although there are many variations within these basic classifications. Examples of crystals from the seven systems are shown on the opposite page as diagrams. In the descriptions of minerals in the following pages, you will find the system to which each mineral belongs is listed in the caption.

The seven crystal systems

Cubic system

Tetragonal system

Orthorhombic system

Triclinic system

Monoclinic system

Trigonal system

Hexagonal system

Growing Crystals

You can grow crystals at home if you follow these instructions. The crystals behave just the way they do in nature and will seem to grow. What they are actually doing is to re-form themselves (or crystallize) out of a liquid. All crystals are solids, but to make crystals you must start with a liquid.

Frosted windows

If it is very cold in your bedroom at night, you may have woken up to find beautiful frost patterns all over the glass. This is where the water vapor, that normally appears as droplets of condensation, has frozen. The same thing happens inside cars when it is very cold. You can make this happen any time and without getting the room cold!

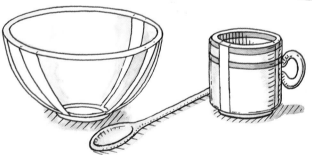

1 **Borrow** a mixing bowl, a mixing spoon, and a cup from the kitchen. (Ask permission first!)
2 **Fill the cup with borax crystals** and put them into the bowl. (You can buy borax (washing soda) from a supermarket or grocery store.)
3 **Fill the cup with hot wate**r from the tap and add it to the crystals in the bowl.

4 **Stir gently** until most of the crystals disappear.
5 **Dip a sponge or cloth into the liquid** and wipe it gently over a window. It does not matter which way you wipe, but try not to go over the same patch twice.

6 **Wait for about 20 minutes** and see what happens to the window.
7 **If you add some blue food dye to** the liquid, it will make the frost crystals look even colder. Try other colors as well (but not all at once) to see how the frost changes.

8 **You can do this experiment with other things as well.** Try Epsom salts (buy them from a drug store) or bath salts. Does the frost have a different pattern with a different substance?

Crystal sculptures

Crystals will form themselves around any shape offered to them. You can make use of this behavior to make crystal sculptures.

1 **Buy a pack of pipe cleaners** and cut them in half with a pair of pliers.

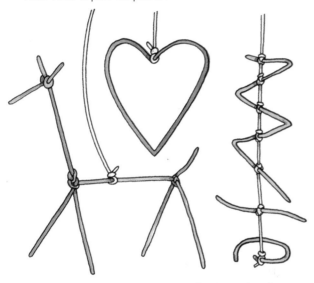

2 **Twist them together** to make an animal, a tree, or a shape (see the picture for some ideas). Tie a thread to the top of the sculpture.

3 **Borrow** a mixing bowl and mixing spoon from the kitchen (ask permission first).

4 **Measure out 4 fl.oz of hot water** from the tap, and pour it into the bowl.

5 **Weigh out 8 oz of Epsom salts** and pour them into the water. (You can buy Epsom salts from a supermarket or a drug store.)

6 **Stir gently** until the Epsom salts are dissolved; then add four or five drops of food dye to the mixture. Pour the mixture into a wide-mouthed glass jar and leave it to cool.

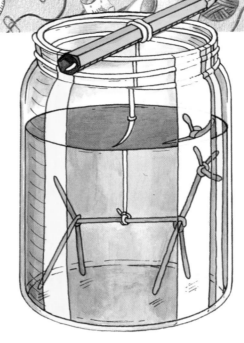

7 **Put the jar on a sunny window sill** or in a warm place. Tie the other end of the thread on the sculpture to a pencil and balance this across the mouth of the jar so that the sculpture hangs in the solution.

8 **Leave in the warm place for 2–3 days** while the crystals form. When you take the sculpture out, treat it very gently so that the crystals do not break off.

Identifying Minerals

You can identify some minerals just by looking at them. But many minerals cannot be completely identified in this way, and there are some other simple tests you can do which can help to get an accurate result.

1 You can test the mineral for its **hardness**.
2 You can test its **streak color**.
3 You can also measure its **specific gravity**.

Each mineral shown in this book has a caption that tells you which crystal system (or family) it belongs to, its streak color, its specific gravity, and a bar scale showing its hardness.

The crystal families are shown on pages 40–41 in diagram form. Have a look at the rest of these two pages to see how to carry out tests for hardness, specific gravity, and streak.

1 Testing the hardness

In 1822 Friedrich Mohs, a German chemist, worked out a set of ten sample minerals for hardness testing. Each mineral can be scratched by any mineral with the next higher number on the list. Diamond (10) scratches everything else. Quartz (7) will scratch window glass.

All the test substances listed above are easy to find. You may be able to find a diamond in an old glass-cutter. Experts use special hardness testers with a splinter of each mineral set in metal holders.

Mineral	No.	Scratched by
Talc	1	fingernail (easy)
Gypsum	2	fingernail
Calcite	3	Copper coin
Fluorite	4	Penknife blade (easy)
Apatite	5	Penknife blade
Orthoclase	6	Steel file (easy)
Quartz	7	Steel file
Topaz	8	Steel file (difficult)
Corundum	9	Steel file (very difficult)
Diamond	10	Scratches every other substance

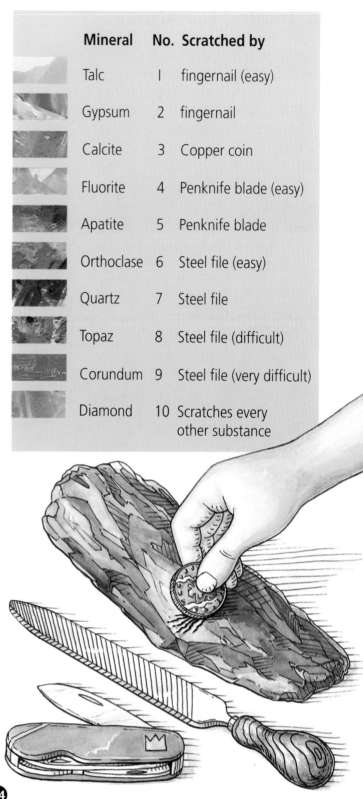

Hardness bar scale

There is one of these bar scales alongside each mineral shown on pages 46 to 75. The harder the mineral, the higher the color rises.

2 Testing the streak

The streak test gives the true color of a mineral when powdered, which may be quite different from the color of the crystal. You can do this test on the back (the unglazed side) of an ordinary wall tile. Experts use a special, rough, porcelain plate.

When you scrape the mineral across the tile it will leave a streak of fine powder behind. You may be surprised at the difference in color. For example, pyrite is brass-colored and often mistaken for gold; but its streak is black (gold makes a gold streak). Spinel crystals can be red, blue, brown, or black,

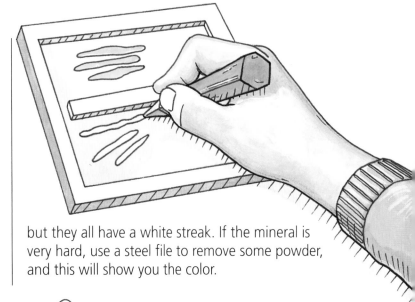

but they all have a white streak. If the mineral is very hard, use a steel file to remove some powder, and this will show you the color.

3 Measuring specific gravity

Specific gravity is another name for relative density and is an important means of identifying minerals. You are comparing the weight of your mineral specimen to the weight of water, which is always the same and which has a density (specific gravity) of 1.

To measure specific gravity you need a hanging scale with a hook (buy it in a hardware store).

1 **Tie the mineral up in a sling** and weigh it dry (see left-hand picture). Write the weight down **(A)**.

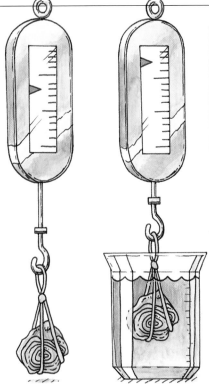

2 **Put a glass or jar of water under the scale**.
3 **Hang the mineral** in the water in the sling (see right-hand picture).
4 **Write down the weight** of the mineral in the water **(B)**.
5 **Work out the specific gravity** using these sums:
First: weight in air **(A)** – weight in water **(B)** = volume
Second: weight in air **(A)** ÷ volume = specific gravity

With a little practice you can get the specific gravity of specimens correct to two decimal places—this is good enough for identification purposes.

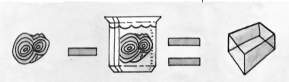

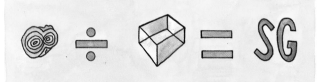

Igneous Minerals

Analcime

Analcime is found as a secondary mineral in many igneous rocks. Its crystals are transparent or translucent. They may be colorless, white, gray, or have pink or yellow tinges. Analcime is found all over the world. There are notable deposits in New Jersey, in Quebec in Canada, and in Italy, Germany, and Scotland in Europe. The mineral's name comes from a Greek word meaning weak, because when crystal is rubbed it develops a weak electrical charge. It is mainly of interest to scientists and collectors.

Chemical composition: $NaAlSi_2O_6.H_2O$
Crystal system: Cubic
Hardness: 5–5.5 – Specific gravity: 2.22–2.29 – Streak: White

Apophyllite

Apophyllite is a secondary mineral in **basalt** and other igneous rocks. It is found in Colorado, New Jersey, Virginia, and Canada, usually as large pale green crystals. Pale pink crystals have been found in Mexico and Germany. The best crystals come from the Bombay area of India. The name apophyllite comes from a Latin word meaning to strip leaves, because the mineral flakes into pieces when heated. It has no commercial uses.

Chemical composition: $KCa_4Si_8O_{20}(F,OH).8H_2O$
Crystal system: Tetragonal
Hardness: 4.5–5 – Specific gravity: 2.3–2.5 – Streak: White

Copper

Copper is one of the most useful metals. It is found in ores combined with **sulfur**, and more rarely as native (pure) metal. The finest native copper comes from the Keeweenaw Peninsula on Lake Superior, and from Arizona, Michigan, Europe, Namibia, and China. It is easily shaped by being drawn into threads or beaten, and it is a first class conductor of electricity and heat. Its name comes from the Greek word for the island of Cyprus, an early source of the metal.

Chemical composition: Cu
Crystal system: Cubic
Hardness: 2.5–3 – Specific gravity: 8.9 – Streak: Shining pale red

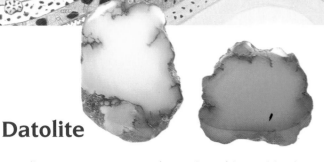

Datolite

Datolite occurs as a secondary mineral in cavities in **basalt**, **granite**, and other igneous rocks. It comes in many transparent or translucent colors, from red through pink, brown, yellow, green to white and colorless. There are major deposits in New Jersey, Massachusetts, and in the Lake Superior region where it is found in basalt flows, and also in Mexico and in Germany and Italy in Europe. The name comes from a Greek word meaning to divide. Datolite is a source of the element boron. Large crystals are occasionally used as gemstones.

Chemical composition: $CaBSiO_4(OH)$
Crystal system: Monoclinic
Hardness: 5–5.5 – Specific gravity: 3
Streak: Colorless

Diamond

Diamond is the hardest mineral known. It may be colorless, yellow, green, blue, or pink. It is often found in pipe-shaped deposits of a rock called kimberlite. The pipes were once the openings of volcanoes. It has also been found in gravel, washed out from kimberlite pipes. The main sources are Australia, southern and western Africa, Siberia, and Venezuela. Diamond is pure carbon, and if heated turns into **graphite**. Its name comes from a Greek word meaning indestructibility. The finest stones are used as jewelry. Tiny diamonds are used in industry for cutting and drilling.

Chemical composition: C
Crystal system: Cubic
Hardness: 10
Specific gravity: 3.52
Streak: Ash-gray

Magnetite

Magnetite is an important source of iron. It is black and magnetic, and sometimes forms a lodestone (a natural magnet). It is found all over the world in igneous and metamorphic rocks, and in sands. There are large deposits in the Adirondacks, Utah, and Wyoming, and in Sweden, Russia, and South Africa. Fine crystals are found in French Creek, Pennsylvania and Franklin, New Jersey. The name comes from Magnesia, a district in northern Greece where it was once found.

Chemical composition: $Fe^2+Fe^3+2O_4$
Crystal system: Cubic
Hardness: 6 – Specific gravity: 5.2 – Streak: Black

Natrolite

Natrolite is found in cavities in **basalt**, **pegmatite**, and other igneous rocks. Its slender, square needle-like crystals are colorless or white. Huge crystals have been found at Asbestos in southern Quebec, and at Bound Brook, New Jersey, where some can be cut as gemstones. Other sources are in Europe, India, and Australia. Its name comes from natron (sodium), its main ingredient.

Chemical composition: $Na_2Ca_2Si_3O_{10}.2H_2O$
Crystal system: Orthorhombic
Hardness: 5.5 – Specific gravity: 2.2–2.26 – Streak: White

Igneous Minerals

Olivine

Olivine is the name of a group of minerals, compounds of magnesium, iron, and silica. They range from Forsterite (magnesium silicate) to Fayalite (iron silicate). The variety called Peridot is valued as a gemstone. Olivines are found all over the world in igneous rocks. Their name comes from their dark olive-green color. Fine, bright peridot comes from Arizona, Hawaii (where they are bright green), German, and Norway in Europe, St John's Island in the Red Sea, and Myanmar. Rocks containing a lot of olivine are a source of magnesium.

Chemical composition: Mg_2SiO_4 to Fe_2SiO_4
Crystal system: Orthorhombic
Hardness: 6.5–7
Specific gravity: 3.22–4.29; peridot approximately 3.34
Streak: Varies

Sodalite

Sodalite is found in igneous rocks such as **syenite**, volcanic rocks, and altered **limestones**. It varies from colorless to dark blue, occasionally reddish, or greenish. It occurs in Arkansas, Maine, Massachusetts, and Montana. It is also found in Canada, South Africa, Brazil, and in the lava flows of Vesuvius and other Italian volcanoes. Large masses are used as polished slabs or for carving. Its name comes from its main ingredient, sodium.

Chemical composition:
$Na_8Al_6Si_6O_{24}Cl_2$
Crystal system: Cubic
Hardness: 5.5–6
Specific gravity:
2.14–2.40
Streak: Colorless

Pyrrhotite

Pyrrhotite is a form of iron sulfide, but with comparatively little iron in it. True iron sulfide (FeS), called troilite, is found in meteorites (see pages 36–37). Good crystals are found in the western United States, Brazil, Mexico, Europe (particularly in parts of Scandinavia, Italy, Germany, Austria, Serbia, and Bosnia), and also in China. Pyrrhotite's name comes from a Greek word meaning reddish, and refers to its color, which is bronze-yellow to brown. It is found among igneous rocks along with other sulfides, such as **pyrite** and **chalcopyrite**. It has no commercial use.

Chemical composition: $Fe_{1-x}S$
Crystal system: Monoclinic and hexagonal
Hardness: 3.5–4.5 – Specific gravity: 4.69
Streak: Dark grayish black

Zircon

Zircon is a gemstone with a wide range of colors, stretching from colorless (when it has been used as a substitute for **diamond**) through yellow, brown, red to green. Zircons are found in granites, or in alluvial (river) deposits. The best gem quality stones come from South-East Asia, especially Cambodia and Thailand. Other stones come from Norway, Sweden, the Ural Mountains, India, Sri Lanka, Australia, and Nigeria. The name is derived through Arabic from a Persian word meaning gold-colored.

Chemical composition: $ZrSiO_4$
Crystal system: Tetragonal
Hardness: 7.5 – Specific gravity: 4.6–4.7 – Streak: Colorless

The minerals on pages 49–51 are secondary minerals, often found near hot springs.

Arsenopyrite

Arsenopyrite is iron arsenic sulfide. It is the main source of the poisonous chemical element, arsenic, which has several industrial uses. If you hit lumps with a hammer they give off sparks and a smell like garlic. It is found worldwide in veins in metal mines, and also with **gold**, **silver**, and nickel. A main source is the Mother Lode in California. Good crystals have been found in Cornwall in England, and in Norway, Sweden, Germany, and Italy. Its name comes from its ingredients.

Chemical composition: FeAsS
Crystal system: Monoclinic
Hardness: 5.5–6 – Specific gravity: 5.9–6.2 – Streak: Black

Cassiterite

Cassiterite is tin oxide, and is the principal ore of tin. It is found as crystals or as masses. The main commercial sources are in Bolivia, China, Indonesia, Malaysia, and Russia. Fine crystals have been found in Britain. There is very little in the United States; some has been found in a few locations in Montana and in Washington. The name comes from the Greek word for tin.

Chemical composition: SnO₂
Crystal system: Tetragonal
Hardness: 6–7
Specific gravity: 6.99
Streak: White or brownish

Bournonite

Bournonite is an ore of antimony, **copper**, and lead, which are its main ingredients. It is black to very dark gray, with a metallic luster. It is common, and is found in hydrothermal veins, often with **galena**, **quartz**, **silver**, and other minerals. Large crystals have been found at Park City, Utah, and in Arizona, California, Colorado, and Montana. Other sources include Mexico, Cornwall in Great Britain, Germany; and Australia. Crystals up to 4 ins across have come from Bolivia. It is named for the French crystallographer Jacques Louis de Bournon.

Chemical composition: PbCuSbS₃ – Crystal system: Orthorhombic
Hardness: 2.5–3 – Specific gravity: 5.8–5.9 – Streak: Steel-gray

Galena

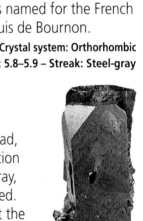

Galena is the chief ore of lead, and often occurs in association with **silver**. It forms soft, gray, cubic crystals, easily identified. Galena is found throughout the world, in widely differing types of deposits including **limestones** and hydrothermal veins. Fine specimens come from Joplin, Missouri, from Kansas, and Oklahoma. It is also found in England, Germany, Sardinia, and the Alpine areas of Italy. The main commercial sources are in Australia, Russia, the United States, and Canada. The name comes from the Latin word for lead ore.

Chemical composition: PbS – Crystal system: Cubic
Hardness: 2.5–2.75 – Specific gravity: 7.58 – Streak: Gray

Igneous Minerals

Gold

Gold is one of the softest metals. It is valued because it does not corrode. It can be easily hammered or drawn into shape. It is most familiar in the form of native metal—grains or nuggets—but it also occurs, very rarely, as a variety of beautiful crystals. Its color ranges from orange-red to white. It is found in hydrothermal veins, near volcanic vents, or in river beds. There are small deposits in Wales, Italy, and Hungary, but the leading producers are South Africa, Russia, China, Canada, the United States, Brazil, and Australia. Its name comes from the Old English word for gold.

Chemical composition: Au
Crystal system: Cubic
Hardness: 2.5–3
Specific gravity: 15.3–19.3
Streak: Same as the color

Pectolite

Pectolite is found in cavities in **basalt** and other igneous rocks. It is colorless to pale blue. It often forms needle-like crystals which can prick you if handled. Good, pale crystals are found in New Jersey, and Quebec and Ontario in Canada. Other sources include Italy and the Kola Peninsula in Russia. A deeper blue variety from the Dominican Republic, called Larimar, is used as an ornamental stone, but pectolite has no other uses. Its name comes from a Greek word meaning compact, because it is compact in structure.

Chemical composition: $NaCa_2Si_3O_8OH$
Crystal system: Triclinic
Hardness: 4.5–5 – Specific gravity: 2.74–2.88 – Streak: White

Prehnite

Prehnite is found in cavities and veins in igneous rocks such as **basalt** and **granite**, in the metamorphic rock **gneiss** and in metamorphosed **limestones**. It is named for the Dutch soldier Colonel Hendrik von Prehn, who first collected it in South Africa in the 1700s. Fine white crystals are found in California, New Jersey, Quebec, and Europe, especially Italy and France.

Chemical composition: $Ca_2Al_2Si_3O_{10}(OH)_2$
Crystal system: Orthorhombic
Hardness: 6–6.5 – Specific gravity: 2.9–2.95 – Streak: Colorless

Siderite

Siderite is iron carbonate. It is nearly half iron, and is an important ore of that metal. It is a common mineral, with worldwide distribution. Its transparent to translucent crystals are green, yellow, or yellowish-brown. It occurs in many rock formations, including sedimentary layers along with coal seams, hydrothermal veins, and **basaltic** rocks. Good crystals occur in Idaho, and there are large deposits in Pennsylvania, Connecticut, and Greenland. There are also deposits in England, France, Germany, Austria, Romania, Italy, and Spain. Its name comes from the Greek word for iron.

Chemical composition: $FeCO_3$ – Crystal system: Trigonal
Hardness: 3.5–4.5 – Specific gravity: 3.96 – Streak: White

Linarite

Linarite is lead copper sulfate. It was first found at Linares in Spain, for which it is named. It occurs in lead and **copper** deposits, as crusts, masses, or fine deep blue crystals. It is often mistaken for the more common **azurite**. The best crystals come from the Mammoth Mine, Tiger, Arizona, and are more than 4 ins long. Linarite is also found in California, Montana, New Mexico, and Utah, as well as in Argentina, Great Britain, Germany, and Australia.

Chemical composition: $PbCu(SO_4)(OH)_2$
Crystal system: Monoclinic
Hardness: 2.5 – Specific gravity: 5.35 – Streak: Pale blue

Stibnite

Stibnite is antimony sulfide, and is the most important ore of the chemical element antimony. It forms lead-gray, slender metallic crystals which are much sought after by collectors. It occurs in hydrothermal veins and in hot springs. The finest crystals came from the Ichinokawa mines in Japan, but these are now almost worked out. Others come from France, Italy, and Romania. There are major deposits in Idaho and China, with others in California, Borneo, Bolivia, Mexico, and Peru. The name comes from a Greek word referring to stibnite's use as eye makeup.

Chemical composition: Sb_2S_3
Crystal system: Orthorhombic
Hardness: 2
Specific gravity: 4.63
Streak: Gray

Witherite

Witherite occurs in hydrothermal veins, often with **barite** and **galena**. It forms colorless white to pale yellow, or green translucent crystals, or exists as masses. It is found in Castle Dome, Arizona and Platina, California, and also Britain, Siberia, and Japan. Witherite is an important source of barium, which has many uses in industry. It is named for an English physician and botanist, William Withering.

Chemical composition: $BaCO_3$
Crystal system: Orthorhombic
Hardness: 3–3.5
Specific gravity: 4.29
Streak: White

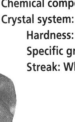

Igneous Minerals

The minerals on this spread are often found with sulfur deposits or near salt lakes.

Argentite

Argentite is silver sulfide, and is a major ore of silver. Its name comes from the Latin word for **silver**. It is found with native silver and **galena**. There is a major deposit in the Comstock Lode in Nevada. It is also found in Colorado, Ontario in Canada, and in Mexico. Large crystals are found in Norway, Germany, the Czech Republic, and Sardinia. Argentite only crystallizes above 355° Fahrenheit. At normal temperatures it occurs in a chemically identical form called Acanthite.

Chemical composition: Ag_2S – Crystal system: Cubic
Hardness: 2.5–3.5 – Specific gravity: 7.2–7.3 – Streak: Silver

Barite

Barite is a very heavy mineral, and an old name for it was Heavy Spar. (The weight of specimens is a good clue for identifying them.) Barite is the commonest ore of barium, which has many uses in industry. It is found worldwide in hydrothermal veins or in **limestone** and other sedimentary rocks. It can be colorless, white, yellow-brown, or blue, and is transparent or translucent. Gem-quality yellow crystals are mined in South Dakota, and Arizona. Huge crystals have been mined in south-western and northern England; it is also found in northern Italy, Sardinia, and the Sahara desert. The name comes from a Greek word meaning heavy.

Chemical composition: $BaSO_4$ – Crystal system: Orthorhombic
Hardness: 3–3.5 – Specific gravity: 4.5 – Streak: White

Chalcocite

Chalcocite is an important source of **copper** and is found with other copper minerals. It is a dark lead-gray in color. The most common form is as large dull gray aggregates. Crystals are rare, but some fine crystals have been found at Bristol, Connecticut and Butte, Montana; and also in Cornwall, England, and in France. Major sources of the mineral are in Australia, Namibia, Chile, Mexico, Peru, and Russia. Its name comes from the Greek word for copper.

Chemical composition: Cu_2S – Crystal system: Monoclinic
Hardness: 2.5–3 – Specific gravity: 7.2–7.4
Streak: Blackish lead-gray

Chalcopyrite

Chalcopyrite is copper iron sulfide, and is the most common **copper** mineral. It is brassy yellow in color, but tarnishes. It is found with other sulfide deposits, often in hydrothermal veins (those created by high temperatures and water). Fine crystals are found at Ellenville, New York, French Creek, Pennsylvania, and in Russia, Turkey, and China. Chalcopyrite is also found in Savoy in France. There are large deposits in Norway, Germany, Bosnia, Serbia, Italy, and Spain. The name comes from two Greek words meaning copper and pyrite.

Chemical composition: $CuFeS_2$
Crystal system: Tetragonal
Hardness: 3.5–4
Specific gravity: 4.1–4.4
Streak: Greenish-black

Cinnabar

Cinnabar is a sulfide of mercury. It is the main ore of mercury, which is the only metal that is liquid at room temperatures. Cinnabar usually forms red, gray, or black masses, but also is found as scarlet crystals. It is commonly found in veins near recently formed volcanic rocks. Fine crystals come from Mount Avala in Serbia. There are major mercury mines in Serbia, Italy, and Spain. Cinnabar is also found in Algeria, California, Peru, and China. The name comes originally from the Persian (Iranian) word for this mineral.

Chemical composition: HgS
Crystal system: Trigonal
Hardness: 2–2.5
Specific gravity: 8.09
Streak: Scarlet to reddish-brown

Colemanite

Colemanite is one of the main ores of the chemical element boron. It forms colorless or yellowish crystals, and also masses. The best crystals come from Turkey and Kazakhstan. Colemanite is found in salt-lake deposits. It is extensively mined in California, especially in Death Valley, and also in Argentina, Chile, Kazakhstan, and Turkey. Boron is used in the chemical industry and in nuclear reactors. It is named for William Tell Coleman, who founded the American borax industry.

Chemical composition:
$Ca_2B_6O_{11}.5H_2O$
Crystal system: Monoclinic
Hardness: 4.5
Specific gravity: 2.42
Streak: White

Gypsum

Gypsum is formed through the evaporation of salty water, and also occurs in sedimentary and volcanic deposits. It is found in many parts of the world. It forms crystals of various shapes, colorless to pale yellow, green or brown. Huge crystals are found in Sicily and other areas of Italy. In the western American and North African deserts it forms rose-shaped crystals, tinged with red from sand, and known as Desert Roses. It is used to make Plaster of Paris. A variety called Alabaster is used for sculpture. The name gypsum comes from the Greek word for chalk.

Chemical composition: $CaSO_4.2H_2O$
Crystal system: Monoclinic
Hardness: 2 – Specific gravity: 2.32 – Streak: White

Sulfur

Sulfur is one of the chemical elements that occurs in the native state. It often occurs as a result of volcanic activity, as at the fumaroles in Yellowstone National Park and on the slopes of Mount Vesuvius in Italy. There are large sulfur beds in Louisiana and Texas. It forms beautiful yellow crystals, which are transparent or translucent. The finest crystals are found at Agrigento, Sicily. Sulfur's name comes from the Latin word for the element.

Chemical composition: S – Crystal system: Orthorhombic
Hardness: 1.5–2.5 – Specific gravity: 2.07 – Streak: White

All the minerals found in the next four pages are most usually found with a particular sort of granite called pegmatite (see pages 14–15).

Apatite

Apatite is the name of a group of common phosphate, arsenate, and vanadate minerals. The most common is Chlorapatite, basically made up of calcium phosphate with chlorine. Apatite is found in volcanic and other igneous rocks, some sedimentary rocks, and in metamorphic rocks. It varies from colorless to yellow, brown, green, blue, or red. It is used in the chemical industry, and some fine crystals are used as gemstones. Violet crystals come from Germany, while blue crystals are found in Maine and in Australia. The name comes from a Greek word meaning deceit, because apatite was commonly confused with other minerals.

Chemical composition: $Ca_5(PO_4)_3(F.Cl.OH)$ and variations
Crystal system: Hexagonal
Hardness: 5 – Specific gravity: 3.17–3.23 – Streak: White

Beryl

Beryl is beryllium aluminum silicate. It occurs worldwide in the igneous rock **pegmatite**. It includes the gemstones Aquamarine, which is colored blue by traces of iron, and Emerald, which is colored green by chromium. Other colors include pink (called Morganite and found in California), red (colored by manganese and found in Utah), and yellow (called Helidor). Beryl is also found in New Mexico, North Carolina, and South Dakota. The finest emeralds come from Colombia and the best aquamarines from Brazil. Beryl crystals can weigh as much as 25 tons. It is the main source of beryllium, used in rockets and artificial satellites. The name comes from the Greek name for the mineral.

Chemical composition: $Be_3Al_2(SiO_3)_6$
Crystal system: Hexagonal
Hardness: 7.5–8 – Specific gravity: 2.6–2.9 – Streak: White

Biotite

Biotite is one of a group of minerals called micas. It occurs worldwide in **granites**, **pegmatites**, **gabbros**, **schists**, **gneisses**, and other igneous or metamorphic rocks. It forms black, brown, or dark green crystals, but is normally found in plates or sheets. Very large crystals are found in Brazil, Russia, Greenland, and Scandinavia. It has no industrial uses. It is named for the nineteenth-century French physicist Jean Baptiste Biot.

Chemical composition: $K(Mg,Fe^{2+})_3(Al,Fe^{3+})Si_3O_{10}(OH,F)_2$
Crystal system: Monoclinic
Hardness: 2.5–3 – Specific gravity: 2.7–3.4 – Streak: Colorless

Ilmenite

Ilmenite is iron titanium oxide. It is one of the principal ores of the metal titanium. It occurs as aggregates, or as flat, black to dark brown crystals. It is found in **pegmatite** and volcanic rocks, metamorphic rocks, and in sands. There are very large deposits in Florida, Canada, Norway, and Russia, and also in Brazil, and India. Fine crystals come from Italy, Norway, and Switzerland. It is named for the Ilmen mountains in Russia.

Chemical composition: $Fe^{2+}TiO_3$
Crystal system: Trigonal
Hardness: 5–6 – Specific gravity: 4.1–4.8
Streak: Black to yellow or brownish-red

Microcline

Microcline is potassium aluminum silicate, and is one of the potassium group of **feldspar** minerals. It forms twinned crystals colored white, pink, red, or yellow. Microcline occurs worldwide in **pegmatites**, **schists**, and **granites**. A green variety, Amazonite, is found at Pike's Peak, Colorado. Some amazonite is cut and polished as a gemstone. The name comes from two Greek words meaning small and to slant, because ideal crystals contain no right angles.

Chemical composition: $KAlSi_3O_8$
Crystal system: Triclinic
Hardness: 6–6.5 – Specific gravity: 2.4–2.63 – Streak: White

Igneous Minerals

Monazite

Monazite is a phosphate of the radioactive element thorium and of several of the elements known as rare earths. It is the principal ore of thorium and cerium. It forms brown crystals, that are found in **granites** and **gneisses** worldwide. Crystals from **pegmatites** may be large; they occur in North Carolina and Virginia, and in Norway, Brazil, and Madagascar. The name comes from a Greek word meaning solitary, and refers to the mineral's rarity.

Chemical composition: $(Ce,La,Y,Th)(PO_4)$
Crystal system: Monoclinic
Hardness: 5–5.5 – Specific gravity: 4.9–5.3
Streak: Reddish to light yellowish-brown

Muscovite

Muscovite is one of the mica minerals, and one of the most common. It occurs worldwide in igneous and metamorphic rocks and sandstones. Huge crystals have been found in South Dakota and in Canada, Italy, Switzerland, and India. The crystals are transparent or translucent, and range from colorless through gray, brown, yellow, green, violet and rose to ruby red. It is used to make heat and electrical insulation, paper, paint, and porcelain. It is named for the medieval kingdom of Muscovy based on Moscow (in Russia). Sheets of muscovite used for glazing were called muscovy glass.

Chemical composition: $KAl_2(Si_3Al)O_{10}(OH,F)_2$
Crystal system: Monoclinic
Hardness: 2–2.5
Specific gravity: 2.77–2.88
Streak: Colorless

Orthoclase

Orthoclase is potassium aluminum silicate. Like microcline, it is one of the **feldspar** minerals, but forms differently shaped crystals. It occurs worldwide, particularly in **pegmatites**. Its crystals are mostly colorless or white, but may be pale shades of gray, yellow, pink, or blue. Colorado and Nevada are both good sources. Red crystals are found in Germany, Switzerland, and Russia. Fine yellow crystals come from Madagascar. A variety containing thin plates of **albite** forms the gemstone called Moonstone, found in New Mexico, Burma, and Sri Lanka. Orthoclase has many industrial uses, for example as a scouring powder. The name comes from two Greek words meaning straight fracture, because the crystals cleave at right angles.

Chemical composition: $KAlSi_3O_8$ – Crystal system: Monoclinic
Hardness: 6 – Specific gravity: 2.5–2.6 – Streak: White

Rutile

Rutile is titanium oxide, and an important ore of the metal titanium. It occurs in many different environments, including **pegmatites**, hydrothermal veins, sediments, placer (gold-bearing) deposits, and sands. Fine crystals are found at Graves Mountain, Georgia and in Virginia, in the Alps in Europe, and in Australia and Brazil. They range from reddish-brown through red and yellow to black, and may be translucent or transparent. Anatase and Brookite are different forms of titanium oxide. The name comes from a Latin word meaning reddish.

Chemical composition: TiO_2 – Crystal system: Tetragonal
Hardness: 6–6.5 – Specific gravity: 4.23
Streak: Pale brown to yellowish

Spodumene

Spodumene is lithium aluminum silicate, and is one of the pyroxene group of minerals. It is frequently found in **granite pegmatites**. It forms crystals varying from colorless through yellow, pink, and green to violet. Some, found in South Dakota are huge, more than 50 ft long. Spodumene is also found in Connecticut, Maine, Massachusetts, and New Mexico; also in Sweden, Madagascar, Brazil, and Mexico. Gem varieties include Kunzite (lilac), yellow and Hiddenite (emerald-green, only from North Carolina). Spodumene is a source of lithium. Its name comes from a Greek word meaning reduced to ashes, referring to its pale color.

Chemical composition: $LiAlSi_2O_6$
Crystal system: Monoclinic
Hardness: 6.5-7.5 – **Specific gravity:** 3–3.2 – **Streak:** White

Tourmaline

Tourmaline is the name of a group of minerals with complex composition, based on boron, aluminum, and silica. Tourmaline forms in igneous and metamorphic rocks, particularly **pegmatites**. There are six main varieties: Elbaite (rich in sodium, lithium, and aluminum) from Elba in Italy, Russia, Sri Lanka, and California; Dravite (sodium and magnesium) found in Australia; Schorl and Buergerite (sodium and iron) found in granite deposits; Uvite (calcium and magnesium) from New Jersey; and Liddicoatite (calcium, lithium, and aluminum) from Madagascar. The color varies from black to reddish-brown. Most gem tourmaline is Elbaite with the chemical composition as given below. The name comes from the word that the people of Sri Lanka use for this stone.

Chemical composition: $Na(Li,Al)_3Al6(BO_3)_3Si_6O_{18}(OH)_4$ (Elbaite)
Crystal system: Trigonal
Hardness: 7 – **Specific gravity:** 2.98–3.2 – **Streak:** Colorless

Topaz

Topaz, a mineral occurring in **pegmatites**, is best known as a gemstone. Its crystals vary in color from yellow to deep orange-red. The best gems come from Siberia and Brazil, but topaz is also found in California and Utah, in the far west of England, and in the Czech Republic.

Blue topaz is found in Zimbabwe, and dark-yellow crystals in Sri Lanka and Myanmar. Other yellow stones, such as citrine (see **quartz**) are often passed off as topaz. The name comes from the Greek word for the gem.

Chemical composition: $Al_2(F,OH)_2SiO_4$
Crystal system: Orthorhombic
Hardness: 8
Specific gravity: 3.53 – **Streak:** Colorless

Collecting Specimens

There is no better way of studying rocks and minerals than collecting them. But that means you must collect as many specimens as possible in the field, and not from your local rock store. You can't really learn about a rock unless you see where it comes from.

If possible, always go with somebody who knows about rocks and minerals, like a teacher or an experienced collector. They can tell you what you are looking at. Also, join your local mineral society; this is the best way to learn in the field.

Where to go hunting

Your work begins at home, by studying maps and guides to locate good collecting sites (see page 76). The best map is a geological map, whose bright colors show you the location of the various rocks. Looking at old buildings in your neighborhood may give you an idea of the local stone.

Find out where there are old mine dumps. These often have rock specimens from underground. Road cuttings, cliffs, rocky outcrops, and beaches are other good hunting places. **But always ask permission before exploring.**

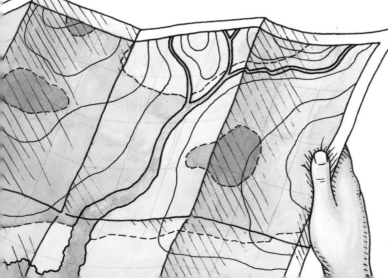

Recording your finds

Try to find loose specimens on the ground—don't break new lumps off the existing rock. Remember that a weathered specimen won't show clearly what the rock is, so be prepared to break it to get an unweathered face to examine.

As soon as you have found a specimen, write down in your notebook where you found it and what you think it is. Then put the specimen in a

plastic bag, together with a brief description on a piece of paper, and seal it. (It is better not to write on the bag itself—your writing might rub off.) Or, you can number the bag and record the details in your notebook. **This is important**—if you don't know where a specimen comes from, it is useless to anyone studying rocks and minerals.

It's a good idea to take photographs of the sites where you find your specimens. If you are taking a close-up of a crystal, always include something in the picture to give an idea of its size—a pencil or a small ruler will do.

Minerals you are most likely to find in the field include non-transparent quartz varieties (page 67), pyrite (page 69), and small garnets (page 72) in metamorphic rock. Leave them embedded in the rock where you found them—don't try to pry them out or you will damage the formations.

What you need

To do your collecting properly you will need some simple equipment, but it must be the right gear. This is what you will need in the field:

1 **Footwear:** walking boots are the best; loose rocks can move, and some are sharp. Strong sneakers (laced up properly) will protect your feet and ankles against injury.

2 **Clothes:** in hot weather make sure you have light clothes to protect you from sunburn. In cooler weather, jeans and a sweater, and waterproof clothes if rain is likely, are best. You also need gloves to protect your hands.

3 **A lightweight backpack:** for your specimens, that leaves your hands free.

4 **A hard hat or other protective headgear:** Rockfalls sometimes occur on cliff faces under which some of the best specimens appear.

5 **Small self-sealing plastic bags:** to put your specimens in.

6 **A small note pad or a roll of 1.5 x 3 inch self-adhesive labels:** they are easier to use for notes about your specimens than trying to write on the bag itself.

7 **A trowel:** for digging specimens out of earth falls. But don't use it to pry specimens out of the rock because you may damage vital mineral groups or fossil specimens. You can find unweathered, loose material very easily on most sites, if you hunt around a little.

8 **A small magnifying glass:** buy one that is ten power (labeled x 10), and wear it on a cord round your neck. A rock store will have one. To use it, hold the glass close to your eye and then bring the specimen close to the glass.

9 **A field notebook with pencils and pens:** you'll need a ballpoint or indelible felt-tip pen if you want to write on your plastic bags.

10 **A camera:** if you take photographs of crystals and rock formations, rather than prying them out, it avoids damaging the environment.

Sedimentary Minerals

Celestite

Celestite is a heavy mineral found in sedimentary rocks, especially **limestones**. It sometimes occurs in igneous rocks or hydrothermal veins. The crystals are translucent or transparent. Some are colorless. Other are pale blue—its name comes from a Latin word which means sky-like. The biggest crystals come from Ohio. Fine blue crystals come from Colorado, and from England, Italy, and Madagascar. Celestite is the main ore of strontium.

Chemical composition: $SrSO_4$
Crystal system: Orthorhombic
Hardness: 3–3.5
Specific gravity: 3.97–4.0 – Streak: White

Hematite

Hematite is the chief ore of iron. It occurs most commonly in thick sedimentary beds, which are found in many parts of the world. One of the largest beds is at Lake Superior in North America. Some hematite forms in volcanic rocks. It is gray to black in color, but when exposed to oxygen it turns red—this is why rust is red. Hematite also occurs as crystals, sometimes as thin flakes forming rosettes. Fine crystals are also found in England, Switzerland, Italy, and Brazil. The name comes from the Greek word for blood.

Chemical composition: Fe_2O_3 – Crystal system: Trigonal
Hardness: 5–6 – Specific gravity: 5.26 – Streak: Deep red

Halite

Halite is common salt, and is often called Rock Salt. It provides beautiful cubic crystals and large masses, but they dissolve in water. It is usually colorless but may be tinged with blue, orange, or purple. It occurs as sedimentary deposits, resulting from the evaporation of ancient oceans or salt lakes. There are large deposits in Louisiana, Michigan, New York, Ohio, and Texas, and in many other parts of the world. There are huge layers of halite deep beneath the Mediterranean and Red Seas—they have saltier waters than either the Atlantic or Pacific oceans. Fine crystals come from Sicily. Salt is essential in our food, and has many uses in industry. The name comes from the Greek word for salt.

Chemical composition: NaCl – Crystal system: Cubic
Hardness: 2.5 – Specific gravity: 2.16 – Streak: Colorless or white

Jadeite

Jadeite is sodium aluminum silicate. It is the brighter of the two minerals known as jade. The other is **nephrite**. Most jadeite is found as pebbles or boulders in streams. Jade has been prized by Chinese jewelers and carvers for thousands of years. The finest, so-called Imperial Jade, is a bright emerald green, but jadeite can also be gray, lavender, or yellow. Most jadeite comes from Tibet and Myanmar, but it also occurs in California, Guatemala, and Italy. Its name comes from a Spanish phrase meaning stone of the side, because it was believed to cure pains in the side.

Chemical composition: $Na(Al,Fe3+)Si_2O_6$
Crystal system: Monoclinic
Hardness: 6.5–7 – **Specific gravity:** 3.33
Streak: Colorless

Nephrite

Nephrite is the other mineral which is described as jade. It is more common and less valuable than **jadeite**. It is a calcium magnesium iron silicate. Nephrite was the main mineral used by the ancient Chinese for carving. Their nephrite came from central Asia, but most nephrite today is mined in New Zealand. The mineral is found in Alaska, California, and Wyoming, and also in British Columbia in Canada, Australia, and Taiwan. It is frequently found in kidney-shaped boulders, and its name comes from the Greek word for kidney.

Chemical composition: $Ca_2(Mg,Fe)_5(Si_4O_{11})_2(OH)_2$
Crystal system: Monoclinic
Hardness: 6–6.5 – **Specific gravity:** about 3 – **Streak:** White

Platinum

Platinum is one of the main precious metals, along with **gold** and **silver**. It is found as a native element, meaning it is not combined with other minerals. It often occurs with gold in placer deposits, having been washed out of igneous rocks. It is rarely found as nuggets or crystals, and is mostly in grains or plates. Among the main sources are rivers in the Ural mountains of Russia, where good crystals occur. It is also found in California and North Carolina, and in Canada, Colombia, and South Africa. Used in jewelry and precision instruments, its name comes from the Spanish word for silver.

Chemical composition: Pt – **Crystal system:** Cubic
Hardness: 4–4.5 – **Specific gravity:** 14–19
Streak: Silvery-white

Turquoise

Turquoise is a pale-blue mineral formed by the action of water on rocks that contain aluminum—though it is generally found in dry regions such as the deserts of Colorado, Nevada, and New Mexico (all important sources), and also in Australia, Chile, and Tibet. It occurs mostly as masses, often in rock cavities, but crystals are rare. Other fine stones come from Iran, Turkestan, and the Sinai Peninsula of Egypt. The name comes from an old French word meaning Turkish, because turquoise was originally imported into Europe through Turkey.

Chemical composition: $CuAl_6(PO_4)_4(OH)_8.4H_2O$
Crystal system: Triclinic
Hardness: 5–6
Specific gravity: 2.6–2.8
Streak: White to pale green

Secondary Minerals

All the minerals shown on pages 62–69 are secondary minerals, which means that they have been changed by chemical reactions within their original rocks, not by movements of the earth's crust.

Anglesite

Anglesite is found in lead ore as a secondary mineral. It is formed by the oxidation of **galena**. Crystal colors range from colorless to brown. Some light-brown or pale-yellow crystals from Westphalia in Germany, and from Morocco and Namibia have been cut as gemstones. Good crystals also come from Idaho, Sardinia, Spain, and Australia. Anglesite is named for the island of Anglesey, off the northwest corner of Wales, where the mineral was originally identified.

Chemical composition: $PbSO_4$
Crystal system: Orthorhombic
Hardness: 2.5–3
Specific gravity: 6.38
Streak: Colorless

Cerussite

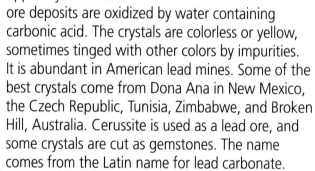

Cerussite is lead carbonate, and is a secondary mineral which forms when the upper layers of lead ore deposits are oxidized by water containing carbonic acid. The crystals are colorless or yellow, sometimes tinged with other colors by impurities. It is abundant in American lead mines. Some of the best crystals come from Dona Ana in New Mexico, the Czech Republic, Tunisia, Zimbabwe, and Broken Hill, Australia. Cerussite is used as a lead ore, and some crystals are cut as gemstones. The name comes from the Latin name for lead carbonate.

Chemical composition: $PbCO_3$
Crystal system: Orthorhombic
Hardness: 3–3.5
Specific gravity: 6.55
Streak: Colorless to white

Azurite

Azurite is a deep-blue mineral found as a secondary mineral in **copper** deposits. It forms large crystals, rosettes or, more rarely, masses. It is often found with malachite. The best crystals are found at the Copper Queen Mine at Bisbee, Arizona, near Lyon in France, in Greece, and in Australia and Namibia. It is occasionally used ornamentally. Its name comes from the Old French word for blue.

Chemical composition: $Cu_3(CO_3)_2(OH)_2$
Crystal system: Monoclinic
Hardness: 3.5–4 – Specific gravity: 3.77 – Streak: Blue

Chalcanthite

Chalcanthite is hydrated copper sulfate, a secondary mineral of **copper**. It is found only in dry areas, because it dissolves in water. Then it may crystallize in a damp mine working, forming crusts or stalactites. It goes powdery when very dry.
It is found in copper mines in Arizona, California, Colorado,

Nevada, Tennessee, and Utah. Good crystals in shades of blue and green are found in Nevada. The biggest deposits are in Chile, where it is a major copper ore, and also in Spain. Its name comes from a Latin word meaning flowers of copper.

Chemical composition: $CuSO_4.5H_2O$
Crystal system: Triclinic
Hardness: 2.5
Specific gravity: 2.28 – **Streak:** Colorless

Chrysocolla

Chrysocolla is a minor ore of **copper**. In masses it is soft, but some chrysocolla contains an appreciable amount of **quartz** and is harder. Chrysocolla forms blue to blue-green crystals. A variety which contains **malachite** is found near Eilat, Israel, and can be used as an ornamental stone. Large masses are found in Arizona and New Mexico, in Morocco, Zimbabwe, and Chile. The name comes from two Greek words meaning golden glue, referring to its former use in soldering pieces of gold together.

Chemical composition: $(Cu,Al)_2H_2Si_2O_5(OH)_4.nH_2O$
Crystal system: Monoclinic
Hardness: 2.0–7 – **Specific gravity:** 2.6
Streak: White when pure

Cuprite

Cuprite is copper oxide. It is a major ore of **copper**, and is found worldwide with other copper minerals. It forms large masses, and also fine, clear red crystals which are found in Arizona. Giant 2 ins crystals from Namibia are sometimes cut as gemstones. Other sources include Russia, France, Sardinia, Bolivia, and Chile. The name comes from the Latin word for copper.

Chemical composition: Cu_2O
Crystal system: Cubic
Hardness: 3.5–4
Specific gravity: 6.14
Streak: Brownish-red

Descloizite

Descloizite is found in many parts of the world, but is rare. It is an important ore of the metallic element vanadium, which is used to make very hard steel. It is found in Arizona, New Mexico, and South Dakota. In Europe, it is found in Austria and in the volcanic lavas of Mount Vesuvius in Italy. Other sources include Argentina, Namibia, and China. Descloizite forms fine, orange to dark reddish-brown or green crystals. It is named for the nineteenth-century French mineralogist Alfred Des Cloizeaux.

Chemical composition: $PbZn(VO_4)(OH)$
Crystal system: Orthorhombic
Hardness: 3–3.5 – Specific gravity: 6.26
Streak: Yellowish-orange to brownish-red

Dioptase

Dioptase is a copper silicate, very popular with collectors because of its dark-green glassy crystals. It is found in the oxidized zone of **copper** deposits. The main sources include Arizona, Chile, the Congo Republic, Namibia, and Kazakhstan. A few crystals are cut to form gemstones. Its name comes from two Greek words, meaning to see through.

Chemical composition: $CuSiO_2(OH)$
Crystal system: Trigonal
Hardness: 5 – Specific gravity: 3.28–3.35 – Streak: Green

Fluorite

Fluorite may be yellow, green, blue, pink, purple, or black. It occurs in veins with lead and silver ores or in joints in Alpine **granites**. Blue John, only found in Derbyshire in England, has bands of violet and white. Fine crystals come from Illinois, Kentucky, and New Hampshire, as well as north-west England, Norway, Germany, Switzerland, and Italy. Other sources include Canada, Namibia, and China. Fluorite is used to make hydrofluoric acid—used in making pottery, glass, and plastics—and in processing bauxite. Its name comes from a Latin word meaning to flow, because of its use as a flux for soldering metal.

Chemical composition: CaF_2
Crystal system: Cubic
Hardness: 4 – Specific gravity: 3.18 – Streak: White

Hemimorphite

Hemimorphite is an ore of zinc. It forms large masses and fibrous crusts in zinc ore deposits. Its comparatively rare white or pale-blue crystals have opposite electric charges at their ends. The name hemimorphite refers to the fact that the crystals have different shapes at opposite ends. Good crystals come from Colorado, New Mexico, New Jersey, and Pennsylvania, and from Mexico. Other sources include the Peak District of Great Britain, Belgium, Austria, and Algeria.

Chemical composition: $Zn_4Si_2O_7(OH)_2.H_2O$
Crystal system: Orthorhombic
Hardness: 4.5–5 – Specific gravity: 3.4–3.5 – Streak: Colorless

Smithsonite

Smithsonite is zinc carbonate. It is named for the chemist James Smithson, founder of the Smithsonian Institution in Washington, DC. Smithsonite occurs as white, green, or blue-green masses, or more rarely as crystals. It is found with other zinc ore deposits. Some of the best material comes from New Mexico. It is also found in Europe, Namibia, Australia, and China. It is polished and used as an ornamental stone.

Chemical composition: $ZnCO_3$
Crystal system: Trigonal
Hardness: 4–4.5 – Specific gravity: 4.3–4.4 – Streak: White

Malachite

Malachite is one of the ores of **copper**. It usually occurs as a green crust on other copper minerals, or as masses. The rare crystals are bright to dark green, with a silky luster. It is found worldwide in the upper oxidized zone of copper deposits. Some of the largest deposits are found in the Ural mountains of Russia, Australia, Zaire, Zambia, and Chile. Fine crystals come from France, Germany, Massachusetts, and Arizona. Malachite is used as an ornamental stone. Its name comes from a Greek word which describes its color.

Chemical composition: $Cu_2(CO_3)(OH)_2$
Crystal system: Monoclinic
Hardness: 3.5–4 – Specific gravity: 4.05 – Streak: Pale green

Rhodochrosite

Rhodochrosite is manganese carbonate. It forms masses and, more rarely, crystals in shades of pink and red. The finest crystals come from the Kalahari region of South Africa, where they are dark orange-pink. Rhodochrosite is also found in Colorado, Montana, and in Peru, and Japan. Other major sources include Germany, Romania, Italy, and Spain. It is used as an ornamental stone and as a gemstone. The name comes from two Greek words describing its color.

Chemical composition: $MnCO_3$
Crystal system: Trigonal
Hardness: 3.5–4 – Specific gravity: 3.7 – Streak: White

Rhodonite

Rhodonite is manganese iron magnesium silicate. It occurs as masses, when its rose-red to pink color is sometimes veined with black manganese oxides, and also as crystals. The finest crystals are found at Franklin, New Jersey, and in Sweden and the Ural mountains of Russia. Rhodonite is also found in Finland, Italy, Brazil, Australia, New Zealand, and South Africa. Cut crystals are prized by collectors; larger masses are used to make ornaments. The name comes from a Greek word for a rose.

Chemical composition: $(Mn,Fe,Mg)SiO_3$
Crystal system: Triclinic
Hardness: 5.5–6.5 – Specific gravity: 3.67 – Streak: Colorless

Serpentine

Serpentine is the name of a group of minerals in which iron, magnesium, or nickel is combined with silica. The snakeskin-like appearance of some serpentine rocks gives the minerals their group name. It is found all over the world in altered igneous rocks. Its many varieties include Bowenite (colored dark green to yellow), Connemara Marble (greenish-white bands), Chrysotile (fibrous form of asbestos, white through gray and yellow to green), and Antigorite (white, green, or greenish-blue). Chrysotile is used for soundproofing and insulation.

Chemical composition:
$A_3Si_2O_5(OH)$
(A = Fe, Mg or Ni)
Crystal system:
Orthorhombic
Hardness: 2.5–4
Specific gravity: 4.1
Streak: Varies

Silver

Silver is one of the precious metals. It is found as wires or scales of pure silver, and also, though rarely, as crystals such as those from Königsberg in Germany. It occurs with other silver minerals such as **argentite**. It is found in many parts of the world, including Arizona, Idaho, Montana, Canada, Germany, and Sardinia in Europe, and Australia. It is found in huge masses in Colorado. Native silver is a rare ore for the metal. The leading producers of silver are Russia, Mexico, Peru, and the United States. People have used silver in many ways for more than 6,000 years. The name comes from an Old English word for the metal.

Chemical composition: Ag – Crystal system: Cubic
Hardness: 2.5–3 – Specific gravity: 10.5 – Streak: Silver-white

Talc

Talc is the softest of all the minerals. It is formed by heat and water from ultra-basic rocks or **dolomites**. It is found in many parts of the world, and forms lumps that vary in color from white through green to gray, and brown. It has a greasy feel. There are large deposits in the United States, Austria, the Pyrenees, India, and China. It is quarried in Sardinia and Italy and then is ground up to make talcum powder. It is also used in making paint, paper, and soap. Slabs of talc are used to line furnaces. A variety called Soapstone is used for carving. The name comes from an Arabic word.

Chemical composition: $Mg_3Si_4O_{10}(OH)_2$
Crystal system: Monoclinic, triclinic
Hardness: 1 – Specific gravity: 2.58–2.83 – Streak: White

Sphalerite

Sphalerite is zinc iron sulfide, and is the main ore for zinc. It occurs with **sulfur** deposits worldwide and is also found in sedimentary rocks in many colors—red, brown, orange, yellow, green, or even colorless. Good crystals come from Arizona, Missouri, New Jersey, and Ohio. Other sources include Switzerland, Hungary, the Czech Republic, Italy, and Spain in Europe, Mexico and China. Large deposits are mined in Austria and Australia. The name sphalerite comes from a Greek word meaning treacherous, because this mineral can be mistaken for the lead ore **galena**, but contains no lead. It is sometimes called Blende, from a German word with the same meaning.

Chemical composition: (Zn,Fe)S
Crystal system: Cubic
Hardness: 3.5–4
Specific gravity: 3.9–4.1
Streak: Pale yellow or reddish

Secondary Minerals

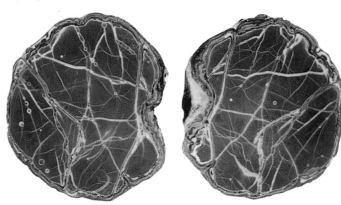

Vanadinite

Vanadinite is lead vanadite chloride, and is an ore of vanadium, a metal used to make very hard steel. It occurs in lead ore deposits. Its beautiful orange-red crystals are sought by collectors. The finest crystals are found in Arizona and New Mexico, and in Carinthia in Austria. The largest come from South Africa. Other sources include Mexico, Russia, Morocco, and China. It is named for vanadium, which in turn was named for a old Norse goddess, Vana-dís.

Chemical composition: $Pb_5(VO_4)_3Cl$
Crystal system: Hexagonal
Hardness: 2.75–3
Specific gravity: 6.88
Streak: White or yellowish

Variscite

Variscite is hydrated aluminum phosphate, and it is formed by water breaking down minerals from igneous rocks such as **pegmatite**. It is found in veins in the surrounding rock. It forms as green nodules or lumps. Crystals are rare. It is found in Arkansas, South Dakota, and Utah, in Austria, and Germany in Europe, and in Western Australia. Its name comes from Variscia, the Roman name for Vogtland, Germany. It is used ornamentally.

Chemical composition: $Al(PO_4).2H_2O$
Crystal system: Orthorhombic
Hardness: 3.5–4.5 – **Specific gravity:** 2.2–2.8 – **Streak:** White

Wulfenite

Wulfenite is lead molybdate. It is a minor ore of the element molybdenum, which has many industrial uses. It forms bright-orange or bright-red crystals, which are valued by collectors. It is found with other lead and molybdenum deposits. Fine, red crystals come from Arizona, Romania, and the Congo. Gray crystals come from the Czech Republic and yellow from Austria. There are other deposits in North Africa, Namibia, Iran, and Queensland, Australia. It is named for the eighteenth-century Austrian mineralogist Franz Xavier Wülfen.

Chemical composition: $PbMoO_4$
Crystal system: Tetragonal
Hardness: 2.75–3 – **Specific gravity:** 6.5–7 – **Streak:** White

Calcite

Calcite has many industrial uses. Its name comes from the Latin word for lime. It occurs as clear or translucent crystals of various shapes. They are usually colorless, but may have pale tints. Calcite occurs all over the world and among all kinds of rocks. Golden-yellow crystals are found in Missouri and Oklahoma. The large clear crystals, known as Iceland Spar, come from Iceland, and have been used for making prisms. Clear crystals have been found in Germany, the Czech Republic, and Italy.

Chemical composition: $CaCO_3$
Crystal system: Trigonal, often twinned
Hardness: 3 – Specific gravity: 2.71–2.94
Streak: White to pale gray

Pyrite

Pyrite is iron sulfide. It is often called Fool's Gold because its cubic, brassy yellow crystals can be mistaken for **gold**. It occurs worldwide in many different environments. Fine crystals are found in Arizona and Colorado, and in Norway, Sweden, Italy, and Spain. A mineral made up of similar elements called Marcasite is used in jewelry. The name comes from the Greek word for fire, because pyrite sparks when struck with steel.

Chemical composition: FeS_2
Crystal system: Cubic
Hardness: 6–6.5 – Specific gravity: 5.0–5.3
Streak: Greenish-black

Opal

Opal is a mineral which does not form crystals. It is made up of regularly-packed stacks of tiny silica spheres, which show a variety of different color effects. Its composition varies with the amount of water in it, and opal should not be allowed to get too dry. Various colored opals are found in Idaho, Nevada, and Oregon, and also in Hungary, Romania, Turkey, and Egypt. The finest black and white opals come from Australia; fire and water opals come from Mexico. The name is from a Sanskrit word meaning precious stone.

Chemical composition: $SiO_2.H_2O$
Crystal system: Amorphous
Hardness: 5.5–6.5
Specific gravity: 2.1
Streak: don't try to test or you'll damage the stone

Quartz

Quartz is one of the most common minerals, forming 12 per cent of the Earth's crust. It is found all over the world in many environments. It occurs as masses, and also as crystals, some of them huge. Good locations include Maine, Colorado, and California. When pure it is colorless, but there are many colored varieties. They include Rose Quartz (pink), Amethyst (purple to violet), Citrine (yellow to golden), Agate, Onyx (banded), and Chalcedony (many patterns and names). A smoky brown variety from Scotland is known as Cairngorm Stone. The name comes from the German word for the mineral.

Chemical composition: SiO_2
Crystal system: Trigonal
Hardness: 7
Specific gravity: 2.65
Streak: Varies

Metamorphic Minerals

Anorthite

Anorthite is calcium aluminum silicate. Like **albite**, it is one of the plagioclase series of **feldspars**, and is found worldwide with **gabbros** and other igneous rocks. The other members of the series, with decreasing amounts of sodium and increasing amounts of calcium, are Oligoclase, Andesine, Labradorite, and Bytownite. Its colorless, white, gray, or greenish crystals are uncommon, but occur in New Jersey, Italy, and Japan. Its name comes from two Greek words meaning not straight; this refers to the uneven way in which the crystal splits.

Chemical composition: $CaAl_2Si_2O_8$ – Crystal system: Triclinic
Hardness: 6–6.5 – Specific gravity: 2.7 – Streak: White

Andalusite

Andalusite is aluminum silicate. It is found in many metamorphic rocks, especially **gneisses**, **schists**, and **slates**. It forms dark green or reddish crystals. They are transparent or translucent, but the variety called Chiastolite is brown and opaque. Andalusite is found in California, Maine, Massachusetts, and Pennsylvania, and in Austria, Spain, Russia, Australia, and Brazil. It is used to make acid-resistant ceramics. The finest crystals are cut as gemstones, including the beige, brown, or green material found in Brazil. It is named for Andalusia, the southern region of Spain, where it was once mined.

Chemical composition: Al_2SiO_5
Crystal system: Orthorhombic
Hardness: 6.5–7.5
Specific gravity: 3.13–3.17
Streak: Colorless

Albite

Albite is sodium aluminum silicate. It is one of the plagioclase series of **feldspars**, an important group of rock-forming minerals. Most albite is white, but specimens are found colored bluish, gray, reddish, or greenish. It is found worldwide, especially with **granites**, **pegmatites**, and igneous rocks. Its crystals are transparent or translucent. Good specimens are found in California and Virginia, and in Switzerland, Austria, and Italy. In industry, albite is used in making ceramics. Its name comes from a Latin word meaning white.

Chemical composition: $NaAlSi_3O_8$
Crystal system: Triclinic
Hardness: 6–6.5
Specific gravity: 2.62–2.65
Streak: Colorless

Axinite

Axinite contains aluminum, boron, calcium, and silica, with small amounts of iron and manganese. It occurs in areas of contact metamorphism, where existing rock is altered by contact with hot volcanic intrusions. The color varies from brown through olive-green, purple, and yellow to colorless. It forms thin, sharp-edged crystals, which are found in California, Nevada, and New Jersey. Some of the best gem quality crystals come from Baja California, Mexico, and France. The name comes from a Greek word meaning axe.

Chemical composition: $(Ca,Mn,Fe,Mg)_2Al_2BSi_4O_{15}(OH)$
Crystal system: Triclinic – Hardness: 6.5–7
Specific gravity: 3.26–3.36
Streak: Colorless or white

Diopside

Diopside is magnesium calcium silicate. It occurs in metamorphosed rocks in many parts of the world including California and New York, and also Scotland, Switzerland, Austria, Finland, Italy, and around Lake Baikal and the Ural Mountains of Russia. Other locations include Brazil, Sri Lanka, and South Africa. Diopside forms crystals varying in color from green to brown. Some of the finest of these are cut as gemstones.

Chemical composition: $CaMgSi_2O_6$
Crystal system: Monoclinic
Hardness: 5.5–6.5
Specific gravity: 3.22–3.38
Streak: White or gray

Corundum

Corundum is aluminum oxide, and is one of the hardest minerals. It comes in many colors. A gray, massive rock called Emery that is widely used as an abrasive is a mixture of corundum with **hematite** and **magnetite**. The colored crystals are valued as gemstones. Those called Sapphires are found in shades of blue, yellow, pink, or dark green because they contain iron. Crystals which are deep red owing to the presence of chromium, are called Rubies. The gemstones come from many countries: the finest rubies and sapphires come from metamorphosed limestones in Myanmar and from placer deposits in Sri Lanka. Emery occurs in Massachusetts, New York, and Pennsylvania, Turkey, and some Greek islands, and also in Australia. The name corundum comes from a Tamil name for ruby.

Chemical composition: Al_2O_3 – Crystal system: Trigonal
Hardness: 9 – Specific gravity: 3.99–4 – Streak: White

Metamorphic Minerals

All the minerals on page 72 belong to a group of minerals called garnets, which occur as crystals in many metamorphic rocks. Several are used as gemstones.

Almandine

Almandine is iron aluminum silicate. Its crystals are deep blood-red or brownish-red. Fine crystals are found in many parts of the United States, especially Alaska and Idaho, as well as in Greenland, Scandinavia, Austria, Italy, and Australia. Most gem almandine comes from India and Sri Lanka. The mineral is ground finely to make abrasive garnet papers. It is probably named for Alabanda, a town in south-west Turkey, an early center for cutting the gems.

Chemical composition: $Fe_3Al_2(SiO_4)_3$
Crystal system: Cubic
Hardness: 7–7.5 – Specific gravity: 4.1–4.3 – Streak: White

Grossular

Grossular is calcium aluminum silicate; the color varies. It is found in California, Colorado, Maine, New Hampshire, and Vermont. Many crystals are used as gemstones. Varieties include Hydrogrossular (green, from South Africa), Tsavorite (emerald-green, from Kenya, and Tanzania), and Hessonite or Cinnamon Stone (yellow, from California and Vermont, Brazil, and Sri Lanka). The name comes from the Latin word for gooseberry, because some stones are the color of the fruit.

Chemical composition: $Ca_3Al_2(SiO_4)_3$
Crystal system: Cubic
Hardness: 6.5–7
Specific gravity: 3.4–3.6
Streak: White

Pyrope

Pyrope is magnesium aluminum silicate. It is found in **peridotites** and **serpentines**, particularly the **diamond**-bearing serpentinites of South Africa, and in Arizona and New Mexico. Pink to purplish-red crystals are found in parts of Europe. A lilac variety occurs in North Carolina, but most gem varieties come from India or East Africa. The name comes from a Greek word meaning fiery.

Chemical composition: $Mg_3Al_2(SiO_4)_3$
Crystal system: Cubic
Hardness: 7–7.5 – Specific gravity: 3.5–3.8 – Streak: Dark red

Spessartite

Spessartite is manganese aluminum silicate and occurs in **gneisses**, **schists**, and **granite pegmatite**s. Fine crystals come from California, Nevada, and Virginia, and from Norway, Germany, Australia, and Brazil. It is named for the Spessart Mountains of Bavaria, Germany.

Chemical composition: $Mn_3Al_2(SiO_4)_3$
Crystal system: Cubic
Hardness: 7–7.5
Specific gravity: 3.8–4.25
Streak: White

Dumortierite

Dumortierite is a hard mineral found in metamorphic rocks containing aluminum. It is blue to greenish, pink, or violet and is translucent. The crystals are rare. Some from Arizona and Brazil are transparent enough to cut as gemstones. The more massive forms are found in Arizona, California, and Nevada. There are deposits in the Lyon area of France, Italy, Brazil, and Madagascar. It is used to make spark-plug ceramics and heat-proof linings for furnaces. It is named for the French paleontologist Eugene Dumortier.

Chemical composition: $Al_7(BO_3)(SiO_4)_3O_3$
Crystal system: Orthorhombic
Hardness: 7 – Specific gravity: 3.26–3.41
Streak: White or bluish-white

Epidote

Epidote is a calcium aluminum iron silicate, found in many metamorphic and igneous rocks. It forms long prism-shaped crystals, green to brown in color. It is occasionally used as a gemstone but has no other commercial value. Fine crystals come from Alaska and Nevada, and from Norway, France, and Austria. Switzerland has yellow and pink crystals of epidote mixed with two similar minerals, clinozosite and piemontite. The name comes from a Greek word meaning to increase.

Chemical composition:
$Ca_2(Al,Fe^{3+})_3(SiO_4)_3(OH)$
Crystal system: Monoclinic
Hardness: 6–7
Specific gravity: 3.38–3.49
Streak: Colorless to gray

Graphite

Graphite is a very soft mineral. It is pure carbon, like **diamond**, but formed under different conditions in metamorphosed rocks. It is black and flexible with a greasy feel. Its most familiar use is as the lead in pencils. The name comes from the Greek word meaning to write. It is black or dark gray, and forms large masses and six-sided crystals. It is found in New York, in the Czech Republic, Madagascar, and Sri Lanka, and many other parts of the world.

Chemical composition: C – Crystal system: Hexagonal
Hardness: 1–2 – Specific gravity: 2.1 – Streak: Black or dark gray

Kyanite

Kyanite is aluminum silicate and generally occurs in **schists**, **gneisses**, and **granite pegmatites**. It forms long blue or green crystals, which are sometimes used as gemstones. It is found in Connecticut, Massachusetts, and North Carolina. In Europe, it is found in Scotland, France, Austria, Switzerland, and Italy. Other locations include Kenya, India, Australia, and Brazil. Kyanite is used industrially in making electrical insulators and high temperature ceramics. The name comes from a Greek word meaning blue.

Chemical composition: Al_2SiO_5 – Crystal system: Triclinic
Hardness: 7.5 across length of crystal, 4.5 along length
Specific gravity: 3.68 – Streak: White or colorless

Metamorphic Minerals

Phlogopite

This strange name comes from a Greek word meaning fire-like, because some of its light brown to yellow crystals have a reddish tinge. It belongs to the mica group of minerals. It occurs as large six-sided crystals, often in metamorphosed limestones. Some of the biggest crystals are found in Ontario and Quebec in Canada, Madagascar, and Sri Lanka. Small flaked deposits of the mineral occur in Sweden, Finland, and Switzerland. Phlogopite is used industrially as an electrical insulator.

Chemical composition: $KMg_3Si_3AlO_{10}(F,OH)_2$
Crystal system: Monoclinic
Hardness: 2–2.5 – Specific gravity: 2.76–2.9 – Streak: Colorless

Pyrophyllite

Pyrophyllite is an aluminum silicate. It rarely forms crystals. It occurs as large masses, with radiating, shell-like shapes. It varies in color from white through shades of gray and green to yellow and has a soapy feel. Large deposits have been found in Arkansas, California, Georgia, and the Carolinas, and in the Ural mountains of Russia, and South Africa. It has several industrial uses. Its name comes from two Greek words meaning fire and leaf, because it flakes when heated.

Chemical composition: $Al_2Si_4O_{10}(OH)_2$
Crystal system: Monoclinic and triclinic
Hardness: 1–2
Specific gravity: 2.65–2.9
Streak: Variable

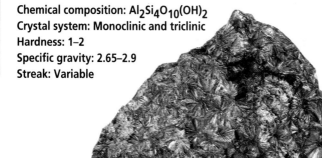

Scheelite

Scheelite is calcium tungstate. Its colorless to yellow crystals occur in contact metamorphic deposits, hydrothermal veins, **pegmatites**, and placer deposits. The best, weighing up to 1 lb, come from Brazil. Scheelite is an important ore of tungsten and economic deposits in masses occur in many places. It is found in Arizona, California, Connecticut, and Nevada, as well as Bolivia, south and east Asia, and Australia. It is named for the eighteenth-century Swedish chemist Karl W. Scheele.

Chemical composition: $CaWO_4$ – Crystal system: Tetragonal
Hardness: 4.5–5 – Specific gravity: 5.9–6.3 – Streak: White

Spinel

Spinel is magnesium aluminum oxide, and is best known as a gemstone. Its crystals come in shades of red, blue, and brown to black. It is found worldwide in metamorphosed **limestones** and in placer deposits. Gem quality crystals are found in Italy, Myanmar, and Sri Lanka. Fine blue crystals come from Montana, and large crystals are found in New Jersey and New York. Its name refers to the shape of some of the crystals, and comes from a Latin word meaning a little thorn.

Chemical composition: $MgAl_2O_4$
Crystal system: Cubic
Hardness: 7.5–8
Specific gravity: 3.6
Streak: White

Staurolite

Staurolite is an iron aluminum silicate with magnesium. It is found in metamorphic rocks, including **schists** and **gneisses**. Its dark to yellowish-brown crystals often occur as twins, forming a cross up to 2 ins long. This is the origin of its name, which comes from a Greek word meaning a cross. The crystals are found in Georgia, New Mexico, North Carolina, and Virginia, and in Scotland, Bavaria in Germany, Switzerland, and Namibia. A very few transparent crystals may be cut as gemstones.

Chemical composition: $(Fe,Mg,Zn)_2Al_9(Si,Al)_4O_{22}(OH)_2$
Crystal system: Monoclinic
Hardness: 7–7.5 – Specific gravity: 3.65–3.83 – Streak: Gray

Wollastonite

Wollastonite is calcium silicate. It occurs in metamorphosed **limestones**. The mineral varies from colorless through white to very pale green. Some of the finest crystals come from New Jersey, Finland, and Romania. Other American sources include California, New York, and Texas. Massive wollastonite is found in north-west France, Germany, and Mexico. It is used in making heat-proof materials and is named for the eighteenth-century English mineralogist William H. Wollaston.

Chemical composition: $CaSiO_3$ – Crystal system: Triclinic
Hardness: 4.5–5 – Specific gravity: 2.87–3.09 – Streak: White

Vesuvianite

Vesuvianite is calcium magnesium aluminum silicate. It was first identified on the slopes of the Italian volcano, Mount Vesuvius, which is how it got its name. It is also called Idocrase, from two Greek words meaning a mixture of forms, because its prism-like crystals vary in shape. The colors vary from yellow through green to brown and reddish. Crystals are found in Switzerland, at various sites in Italy, and in California, where there is a massive variety, called Californite, mixed with grossular garnet. Other important sources include Vermont, Quebec in Canada, Kenya, and Pakistan. Some of the transparent crystals may be cut as gemstones.

Chemical composition: $Ca_{10}Mg_2Al_4(SiO_4)_5(Si_2O_7)_2(OH)_4$
Crystal system: Tetragonal
Hardness: 6–7
Specific gravity: 3.32–3.47; californite is 3.25–3.32
Streak: White

Find Out Some More

Useful Organizations

In addition to the national groups listed below, many communities have local or regional geology clubs. Check with your school librarian, your local public library, the nearest museum, or the earth sciences department of your nearest university, for information on them.

The American Federation of Mineralogical Societies is a hobby-and education-oriented group dedicated to the study and appreciation of earth science; it publishes the *American Federation Newsletter*. Write to: American Federation of Mineralogical Societies, 1203 E. Hillsborough Avenue, Tampa, FL 33603.

The **Geological Society of America** caters primarily to professional and academic geologists, but can be a helpful contact for amateurs as well. Write to: Geological Society of America, P.O. Box 9140, Boulder, CO 80301–9140, (303) 447–2020.

The **Mineralogical Society of America** also caters primarily to professional and academic geologists, but can be a helpful contact for amateurs as well. Write to: Mineralogical Society of America, 1130 17th Street NW, Suite 330, Washington DC 20036 (202) 775-4344.

The **U.S. Geological Survey** is a terrific storehouse of information, including maps and guides. For a listing of publications, write to: Public Inquiries Office, U.S. Geological Survey, 503 National Center, Reston, VA 22092, (703) 648–6892.

In Canada, the **Geological Survey of Canada** in your best starting point. Write to: Geological Survey of Canada, Department of Energy, Mines and Resources, 601 Booth Street, Ottawa, Ontario K1A 0E8, (613) 995–0947.

Places To Visit

You can look for rocks and minerals virtually anywhere, but some locations naturally produce better or more varied specimens than others.

Virtually all state and provincial geologic survey departments publish detailed guides to significant geologic features, including mineral outcroppings and fossil beds, they also publish geologic maps of rock types and formations. Ask your school or local public reference librarian for help in finding these publications—often available free to the public.

Certain areas of the United States are famous for their unusually rich, or varied, specific mineral deposits. **Arizona** may be the most mineralogically varied state of all, with such prizes as petrified wood, turquoise and an abundance of gold, silver and copper. **California** is also geologically complex, with excellent collecting opportunities in San Bernadino and San Diego counties, among other locations.

Pacific beaches, especially those of the Pacific Northwest in **Oregon** and **Washington**, produced wave-tossed specimens like agates, moonstones and jasper. Also in Oregon, obsidian is the attraction at Glass Butte near Prineville.

In the East, the anthracite fields of **Pennsylvania** produce not just hard coal, but also Carboniferous Period fossils, while the state's southeast is famous for garnets, moonstones and amethyst. In **New York**, the rock crystals known as "Herkimer Diamonds" are commonly found in the Adirondack county. Farther east, in **Vermont**, collectors flock to central valleys for rare forms of serpentine. Finally, **North Carolina** has an exceptional store of rocks and minerals, particularly the Appalachians of western North Carolina.

Index & Glossary

Useful Books

The Peterson First Guide to Rocks and Minerals. Frederick H. Pough (Houghton Mifflin Co., 1991) A simplified guide to the most common rocks and minerals of the world.

A Field Guide to Rocks and Minerals. Frederick H. Pough (Houghton Mifflin Co., 1970).

Earth Treasures (Where to Collect Minerals, Rocks, & Fossils in the United States) Allan W. Eckert (4 volumes, Perennial Library, Harper & Row, 1987)

Macdonald Encyclopedia of Rocks and Minerals. Montana, Cresp i& Liborio (Macdonald Orbis, 1983) Has excellent pictures of rock specimens.

Handbook of Rocks, Minerals and Gemstones. Walter Schuman (Houghton Mifflin Co., 1993). A comprehensive guide to specimens of the world.

Mineralogy for Amateurs. John Sinkansas (Van Nostrand, 1964) Still a most useful reference book for beginners.

Index & Glossary

M

magma Molten material in the *mantle* or *crust*, which may solidify to form *igneous rock* 10, 12, 13, 38, 40

Magnetite 47

Malachite 65

mantle The layer of molten rock under the *crust* on which the continental *plates* float 6

Marble 18, 30

marble, Connemara 66

marl 19

mass A shapeless lump of rock or mineral 12, 48, 49, 51, 53, 58, 59, 60, 61, 65, 66, 67, 69, 71, 73, 74, 75

mercury 53

metamorphic rock Any rock which has been altered by volcanic activity or the movement of continents 28–31

meteors, giant 36–37

Meteorite, Iron 37

Meteorite, Stone 37

mica Any one of a group of minerals which splits in one only direction into sheets: eg Muscovite $KAl_2(AlSi_3)O_{10}(OH)_2$). If hit with a sharp point, they produce a six-pointed star around the point of impact 15, 56, 74

Microcline 15, 55

Migmatite 31

MINERALS 38–41
  igneous 46–57

metamorphic 70–75
secondary 62–69
sedimentary 60–61

Mohs Scale Measurement of a crystal's hardness, used to identify it 44

molybdate Salt crystallized from an *acid* containing molybdenum (Mo): eg Wulfenite ($PbMoO_4$) 66

Monazite 56

monoclinic One of the *crystal systems* 41

moonstone 56

morganite 54

mountains, making of 7

mudstone 19

Muscovite 31, 56

N

native mineral A mineral made from only one *element*, such as gold (Au), silver (Ag), copper (Cu), platinum (Pt) or mercury (Hg) 48, 50, 53, 61, 67

Natrolite 47

Nephrite 61

nodule A small rounded lump of a mineral or rock, usually found within a different type of rock 18, 27, 68

nugget A lump of metal, such as gold (Au) 24, 50

O

Obsidian 13

octahedral One of the *crystal systems*, with eight sides 41

oliogoclase 70

Olivine 14, 15, 31, 48

onyx 18, 69

Opal 69

opaque Cannot be seen through, the opposite of *transparent* 70

ore A rock or mineral from which a mineral or metal can be extracted in commercial quantities 14

Orthoclase 15, 56

orthorhombic One of the *crystal systems* 41

oxide Crystallized *compound* of oxygen (O) with another *element*: eg Cassiterite (SnO_2) 49, 55, 56, 59, 66, 71, 74

oxidized Something that has combined with oxygen (O): eg Dioptase ($CuSiO_2(OH)$ 62, 64, 65

P

Pacific Ring of Fire 10

Pangaea 7

panning A mining technique 24

parent rock *Igneous* or *sedimentary rock* from which a *metamorphic rock* is made 14, 30, 31

perlite 13

Pectolite 50

pebbles 8, 18, 26–27

pegmatite Very coarse-grained type of *igneous rock*, often found as *dikes* 47, 54–57, 68, 70, 72, 73

Peridotite 15, 72, 74

Phlogopite 74

phosphate Crystallized

compound of phosphorus (P) with other *elements*: eg Variscite ($Al(PO_4).2H_2O$) 54, 56, 66

placer A *deposit* of sand or gravel in or near a river. It can contain gold (Au), platinum (Pt) and other heavy minerals 24–25, 56, 61, 71

plagioclase See *feldspar* and Albite 14, 15, 70

plates, continental The sections of the *crust* and upper *mantle* which move about carrying the continents 7, 10

Platinum 14, 15, 24, 61

plug, volcanic 10, 12

precious metal Gold (Au), silver (Ag), platinum (Pt) or some other rare metal 50, 61, 67

Prehnite 50

pudding stone 18

Pyrite 69

pyrite nodules 27

Pyrope 72

Pyrophyllite 74

pyroxene Any one of a group of *silicate* minerals; their chemical formulas do not contain water (H_2O): eg Spodumene ($LiAlSi_2O_6$) 15, 65

Pyrrhotite 48

Q

Quartz A very ordinary group of rock-forming silicate minerals 15, 19, 26, 30, 31, 57, 59, 69

Quartzite 31

Index & Glossary

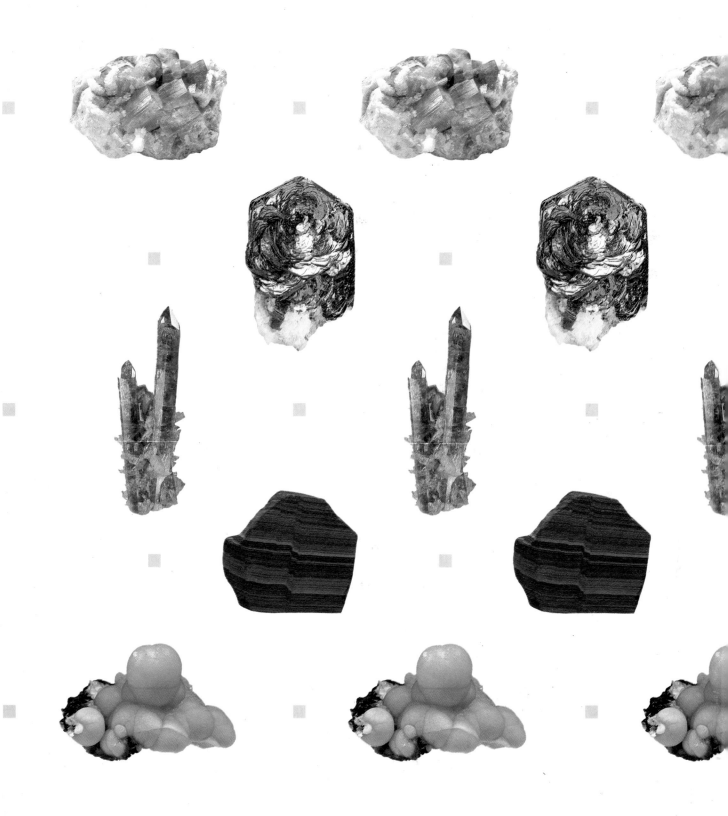